Do BIG!

A SELF HELP GUIDE TO GETTING YOUR GOALS AND BUILDING BETTER HABITS

HANNAH V. HOLMES

To request permissions, contact the author at
hannahvholmes1@gmail.com

Hardcover: 978-1-7343698-9-2
Paperback: 978-1-7343698-8-5
eBook: 978-1-7343698-7-8

Library of Congress Number:

First paperback edition: June 2021

Edited by Courtney James
Cover Art by Adobe Spark
Layout by Jamie Holmes
Photograph(s) by Liv Claire-Brannon

Printed by Harrison Media in the USA

https://www.hannahvholmes.com

To my family
"You don't get to choose if you
get hurt in this world...but you do
have some say in who hurts you.
I like my choices."
—John Green

CONTENTS

CHAPTER 1:

WHO YOU ARE AND WHAT YOU WANT

"Be yourself. Everyone else
is already taken."
—Oscar Wilde

Howdy, I'm Hannah. This is my story. Well, at least the first fifteen years of it. This book has one goal: to help YOU DO BIG and do better than you ever knew you could. I've done some exciting things in my life. Piloted planes, snow skied black diamonds, gone SCUBA diving with sharks in the Great Barrier Reef, and even been interviewed on national television. After training for eight years, I earned my black belt in Taekwondo, finished my first two years' worth of college before I could legally drive a car, and became the first girl in the history of Scouting to earn ALL of the merit badges. I know many teenagers have done even more amazing things, but what I learned along the way was how to go about actually achieving the goals I wanted. And that was step one. Figuring out what you want in the first place. For some, that's the most significant and challenging step of them all.

Once I knew what I wanted, I set goals, developed ways to stay motivated, and methods to manage any opposition. At the same time, I worked to find and sustain my inner happiness in the daily journey, no matter how rigorous or exhausting. Most importantly, throughout my adventures, I was always THINKING BIG. I want to help you do the same, no matter what your goals are and where you want to go in life.

Being able to achieve your goals isn't just dumb luck. You have to build the habits you need to be successful. It takes working hard and working smart at what you want to get there. If this is something you're willing to do, then you're already on the right track to accomplishing your goals and living the best version of the life you want.

Some people seem to know instinctively what they want and how to get there. It's almost like they're born with some precise inner desire. Others need a bit of spark to fuel their ambitions. This book is about striking the match. If you don't have that passion behind what you're working toward, it's almost impossible to find the motivation necessary to get there. Often, this will require doing some soul searching into what you want out of life. Sometimes that inspiration can come from unusual places and in unpredictable ways.

For me, I began asking that BIG question the day I almost lost everything in November of 2011. My family had woken up early to go to a museum in downtown Tampa, about an hour's drive from our house. While my mom was in the kitchen getting snacks and Harrison and Hailey (my two younger siblings) were getting dressed, I climbed into the car. I was only six years old and as I clamored into my car seat the latching mechanism on the seatbelt buckle felt loose. I told my dad who quickly pulled out a father's all-purpose fix-it tool: duct tape. He taped the seatbelt buckle in place, saying he would get it repaired by a mechanic the next day. Soon, everyone was piled in the car and we were off.

We spent the day exploring the exhibits and had a great time. We stayed until closing, then hopped in our old grey Toyota. I was getting sleepy, my brother and sister dozing next to me, the only sounds their slow, peaceful breathing and the tires thumping against the road. Suddenly, a black

Nissan came speeding up next to us and slammed into the left side of our car. My heart seized as my entire world came crashing down around me. The momentum of the crash threw my dad's arm out the car window, and it dragged along the asphalt. I remember my mom in the passenger seat calling out to God to save our family. The car flipped six times and we tumbled into a ditch. Somehow, we landed upright in a pile of smoking metal. My dad jumped out of the car and tried to open the passenger side door, not knowing if his children had survived. As he ripped the door open, all three of us were still sitting in our seats, dazed and confused, but still alive. I will forever remember the shocked look on my father's face as he realized we weren't dead. Suddenly he shouted for us to get out of the car, afraid it would explode. It felt like we were moving in slow motion as he yanked us out of our seatbelts, and we crawled out of the wreck.

The person who hit us had not stopped. Thankfully, another driver who had seen the accident pulled over and called an ambulance. When we emerged from the wreckage, I remember he said he thought we were ghosts. That night my family and I sat on the side of I-4, one of America's deadliest highways, praising God that He had saved us. As we walked to the ambulance, we realized that no one had more than just a few scrapes and bruises. The firefighters on the scene looked at the wreck and said they had never seen anyone survive a crash like that, let alone a family of five. God works in incredible and unique ways. And sometimes, He even uses duct tape.

What I saw, felt, and heard that night still impacts me to this day. It made me realize what a true gift it is to be alive. We don't know how long each of us has before we die. Minutes? Years? Decades? If ever there was a wake-up call to realizing what a precious gift life is, it was when that gift was almost taken. When you think about who you are and what you want in life, it's one of the most meaningful questions you can ask yourself. You have the power to go out and live your life to the fullest. What will you decide to do with the time you have?

This first chapter is dedicated to discovering the real you and figuring out what you want so we can work on getting there. This can take some people their whole lives to figure out. Others never do. That's why starting to think about the things YOU like and what you want to do with your time is so important. The more you understand yourself, the easier it will be to figure out how you can stay motivated, identify what you want, and how you will get there. This doesn't mean your decisions are sealed in concrete. It took me a while to figure out what I wanted but finding that foundation where you know where you stand on specific issues is crucial to becoming the person you want to be. This is especially true in today's world, where it can feel overwhelming with social media, commercials, and magazines telling us how we should dress, act, talk, and look. Take a moment to think about the core of who you are. Imagine knowing precisely what you want, how to get there, and having an unshakeable sense of self-confidence that draws in others. The key to finding this is knowing YOURSELF first. Figure out what makes you wake up ready to work hard, what kind of life you want to have, and who you want to become.

To do this, **ask yourself questions.** This is a great way to reflect and learn more about yourself. Make sure to focus on your answer and why you think that way. The whole point of this is to build confidence in who you are and what you stand for.

Ask yourself:

"Who is my biggest hero and why?"

"What is my idea of success?"

"Where do I want to be in one year? Five? Ten?"

"If I had one day left to live, how would I want to spend it?"

Knowing these answers about yourself is a great way to build the foundation of who you are and figure out what you want. Make sure your answer isn't being determined by someone or something else in your life and that it's what you would put down as YOUR answer. After all, this is YOUR LIFE.

There are a few other ideas to help you root out who you are and the person you want to become.

Take a break from social media. The desire to impress others and become something we're not can be a struggle for all of us. Try taking a break from all social media for a few weeks and comparing what changed inside of you. Did you buy less stuff, get better grades, or spend more time with friends? Do you put more emphasis on how you feel instead of how you look? What does a social media "diet" mean for your overall well-being?

I'm not suggesting you permanently shut off all forms of social media, just that you take a short break for some time away from outside influences so you can focus on figuring out who you are. Work on your internal influencer first.

Look to the past. Think of defining moments where you felt truly comfortable, happy, or proud in your life. Why was that? Were there moments in your childhood that genuinely stood out because of how you were treated? What made that moment special? Was it the moment or the person at that moment with you? Was there a person in your life who influenced you to act, or not to act, in a certain way? Sometimes looking into our past is also a confrontation with people in our lives who left a negative impact. These people can also be powerful teaching tools. Are they showing you the kind of person that you don't want to become?

Reevaluate your relationships. Past or present. Figuring out who you spend time with and why is a great way to figure things out about yourself. Our friends tend to reflect on us, and thus, we can use them as sort of a mirror to see ourselves better. Who your friends are can say a lot about you as a person, so it's essential to hang around people who have your best interests in mind. One of my favorite sayings I try to keep in mind is: "Don't do dumb things with dumb people in dumb places."

Write down a list of strengths and weaknesses. Come up with two lists, one with all the things you're good at and the other list with something you can improve. You can ask a friend or family member you trust to help you if you want. Just make sure you don't take it too personally. Don't be overly critical of yourself either, so make sure to put down two strengths for every weakness. Examples are: "I'm a great leader," "I can paint well," or "I get good grades in math." Examples of weaknesses could be: "I'm not as assertive as I would like," "I want to get better at driving," or "I need to work on being nicer to my sister." Whatever the weaknesses are, they should only be things you want to improve upon and not just because someone else thinks you should. Your personality is one of the things that makes you unique, and instead of trying to change it for others, focus on what you want to improve upon inside yourself.

Make time for yourself to do things you enjoy. If there's something you like to do, make sure to spend time working on it. This could be an instrument, sport, or a new skill. If you're only participating in something because someone else wants you to, you likely won't feel motivated at all. Compare that to something you're interested in accomplishing, and it'll be that much easier to achieve what you want. I love anything to do with the water, so if there's something I know I'm going to dread doing (*ahem* precalculus), I'll use it as a motivator to get what I need to do out of the way. Maybe it's just going for a swim or taking a bath, but there's always some healthy reward I try to build into my day.

Start a journal. This is a great way to learn about yourself. It doesn't have to be a personal revelation, but it can be an excellent way to collect your thoughts in a place where you can go back and look at them later. It's also pretty hilarious later on to read about how you've changed through the years.

Write down what you're grateful for in your life. Showing gratitude isn't just a way to feel thankful for what you have but also a great way to find out where your values are. What you're grateful for shows what's important to you and can help you figure out where your heart is and what matters most. Try writing down at least twenty things and put them in a place you'll see them each day. My list consists of family, friends, various foods (namely pizza), and my home. Each of the items on my list helped me learn something new about myself and analyze how I was spending my time. It'll also help you figure out ways to motivate and reward yourself after achieving your goals and live a happier life.

Establish Your Core Beliefs. Another crucial part of figuring out who you are is knowing your core beliefs. Having a solid set of morals is a great way to help you stand up for yourself. Take some time to think about what you believe in and why. This could be anything from your faith to your political views, but make sure to form your own opinions instead of listening to people or influencers who might just have their own best interests in mind, not yours. There can be a lot of pressure to act, think, dress, talk, or feel a certain way. I encourage you to try tuning out many of these voices since they are often just trying to manipulate you for their benefit.

To become a strong person, you need to be strong on the inside. It starts with what you believe and emanates into the rest of who you are. Finding out your views can be frustrating since it can feel like there are a million different sides to the same argument. It's easy to get so wrapped up in causes that we lose sight of where we stand. And when the ideals no longer align with ours anymore, sometimes we're too invested to care. I'm not saying that you shouldn't support significant causes, but make sure you don't lose sight of your original beliefs in the process. This can apply to all areas of your life. Sometimes it can be as small as changing your music preferences just because that's the genre your crush likes or going along with something you know is wrong because everyone around you is doing it. Whatever it is, little things like this can add up over time to where you might feel lost as to who you are. Sometimes it can be tough to stand up for yourself, especially when it feels like the whole world is telling you something different. This can be great if the people in your life have your best interests in mind, but it can quickly become dangerous if they don't. It's essential to establish healthy boundaries in all areas of your life and know where you stand on specific issues. No one wants to have someone come into their room and take their stuff, or text them at all hours of the night, or have a person's political beliefs shoved down their throat, which is why having boundaries is vital in letting other people know where you stand. This doesn't mean you have to make your mind up right away on who you'd vote for in an election, but there are other things you can do to help establish boundaries. It's important to have a robust set of values because people may try to take advantage of you if you're unwilling to push back and stand up for your beliefs. Some examples could include refusing to drink underage, break the law, curse, or bully others. If it's important to you, then your life and your choices should reflect this. Don't let others push you around and fight to stay true to yourself.

Be Original. This is a call to action. In life, it's easy to go along with what everyone else is doing. But as Mark Twain puts it, "Whenever you find yourself on the side of the majority, it is time to pause and reflect." That's why we need strong individuals like you who dare to think outside the box. Don't be afraid of going your own route in life. I can't stress this point enough. It's OK to be different! Don't try and look, act, or talk like everyone else just because you're afraid of the backlash. God made you the way you are for a reason. It makes me sad to see how much pressure is put on us to try and go along with everyone else (especially on social media) when we should be encouraging independence instead. My goal is not to hate on social media. I think it's a great way to connect with people, share ideas, and promote individuality.

But too often, I see the platforms being used to try and get people to copy trends, plagiarize content, and mock others for having a different set of beliefs than they do. It's creating a whole generation of people drowning in a major identity crisis, and the current is only getting stronger. I believe the only way we can move forward as a generation is if we're willing to set an example in our own lives first. That's why forming your own identity and being comfortable with who you are is so important.

I'm kind of strange. I rarely put on makeup unless I have a public event and usually wear my cowboy boots wherever I go. I'm not up to date on the latest trends, dance moves, and video compilations. I don't fit into any of the "types" of people on social media. That's just who I am as a person, and no one will tell me differently! It hasn't stopped people from pestering or picking on me about how I'm dressed, the way I look, talk, or the boots I'm wearing. Just because I have my own style shouldn't make me such a threat to other people, yet for some reason, it does. I see groups of people who all wear almost the same clothes and all talk in the same manner. It's like they're afraid of straying from the pack and take the "safety in numbers" thing a little too literally. In this world, you have to find your way if you want to succeed. How can you do BIG if you're just going along with what everyone else is already doing, saying, and thinking? Listen to that voice inside of the person you were meant to be instead of random trend setters. Dare to be original and don't just conform to what everyone else is doing. By thinking outside the box, you become a leader and an inspiration for others to follow. The older people get, the more they begin to find their way in life, and the less they care about the pressure coming from others to conform. Just think of how ahead of the game you'll be if you start working on that now. If people try to shun you for who you are, you're hanging out in the wrong crowd. Dance to the beat of your drum, and you'll find that people will begin to follow along.

What You Want

When you look in the mirror in twenty years, who do you want to look back? What kind of person do you want to become? Thinking hard about this is crucial so you can make your goals a reality. If there's anything you could change about yourself now, what would it be? Write down a list of all the characteristics you want to have. Friendly? Confident? Determined? Understand who you are as a person right now so you can figure out who you want to become in the future. Write down the skills and traits. Then, below that, put down concrete ways to achieve those goals. Don't just put down 'being kinder,' but use specific examples of how to be kinder to one person in particular. If your goal is to procrastinate less, put down "stay focused on goals" and list specific ways you can do this.

It's essential to think about the person you want to become to focus on getting there. One of the best ways to do this is by trying new things. When I worked on my merit badges for scouting, many of those skills were far from a typical day's routine. I built a spider robot, made a knife out of steel, welded an iPhone holder, shot and edited a movie, and learned how to drive a motorboat. I learned how to build a website, fly fish, and even repair a tractor. What you learn when trying new things will help you in figuring out your interests. Perhaps, unbeknownst to you right now, looking at the planets through a telescope on top of a remote mountain is just what you need to inspire you to explore space for a career. Either way, the first journey of exploration is inside of yourself. Find out your interests first, and don't be afraid to explore them or try something new. The more time you spend now focusing on what you want and who you want to become, the easier your path will be to follow.

The "American Dream"

When I was growing up in South Florida, my parents worked full-time jobs and we flipped houses on the side. As a child, I would help to paint, carry out trash, and clean yards. It was here that I learned how to work hard for the things I wanted in life. My younger brother Harrison was born just before the market crash in 2008, and I saw firsthand the effects it had on my town. I will never forget going for a walk around my neighborhood and seeing rows of people's possessions thrown out on the street. I realized then that all the material goods people might think are important don't matter. Often in the United States, we're taught that success means having a nice car and a big house. But when looking around, I realized that you can still be successful even if you don't spend money on more stuff. So, when I ask you to dream and do BIG in this book, I'm not talking about ways to keep up appearances or impress your friends. I'm asking you to dig deep and think about what YOU want. Not what your parents, friends, or teachers expect of you, but what will truly make you look in the mirror and feel happy.

Imagine if you had a whole year to do whatever you want. What would that look like for you? I wrote down my hobbies, what my career would look like, and where I'd want to live. No matter who you are, you only get twenty-four hours in a day and a limited number of years on Earth. That's why it's so important to figure out what YOU want in life so you can start working to get there right away. Don't write down the 'stuff' you want. Write down the 'stuff' you want to get out of your life. "What kind of career would be fulfilling?" "What kind of salary do I need to live the lifestyle I want?" "What do I want to accomplish?" "What new things can I learn or do in my free time?" "How can I give back?" Focus on improving yourself before anything else, and you'll begin to find more meaning instead of materials.

Don't worry about the stuff.

It's not going with you.

Defining Success

I'm a "people pleaser" where I try to make everybody happy. But it can come at my expense where I'll do things because someone wants me to instead of figuring out what I want. Trying to make others happy isn't a bad thing. Still, if you struggle with this to the extent that I do, then it's imperative to visualize YOUR life the way YOU want before factoring everyone else into it.

One of the best ways to do this is by writing down your definition of success. I did this by thinking about what would make me wake up every day feeling happy. What shocked me is that it looked nothing like what I had initially thought. For example, when I was little, my "perfect" life involved having ten children (yep, you read that right) and a mansion that curiously looked like Barbie's Dreamhouse. Now I define success a bit differently, so I'd encourage you to dig deep every so often and think about what that looks like for you. Success in this world and success as a Christian can often be opposites. I don't know where you are in your journey with God, and I'm not here to condemn or judge you for it. We're all just trying to find our way in life, and in my experience, that can often be confusing. The world tends to teach us material goods and having a lot of money will bring happiness. Still, many people who listen to the commercial aspects of success end up even more lost and miserable. Often, "success" is portrayed as having a mega-mansion, a big car, a trophy husband/wife, and lots of money to spend on our own comfort. Is this true success? Or is it covering up an emptiness inside?

What if there was another way of living that involved identifying success as beyond material possessions? Well, there is, and it doesn't involve sacrificing your goals or dreams to get there. It incorporates them into your life so you really can have it all.

This is part of the journey that I think is most difficult for people. Pursuit of material possessions is easy. Get a good job, spend as much as you can on stuff, and then show it off to your friends. But is that success? Or is it the illusion of success? Sometimes the easy path isn't always the right one.

For me, I identify success as following your goals with the intent of loving and serving God. Sometimes, this isn't always what we think it would look like either. For instance, God says, "Not everyone who calls out to me, 'Lord! Lord!' will enter the Kingdom of Heaven. Only those who do the will of my Father in heaven will enter. On judgment day, many will say to me, 'Lord! Lord! We prophesied in your name and cast out demons in your name and performed many miracles in your name.' But I will reply, 'I never **knew** you. Get away from me, you who break God's laws.'" (Matthew 7:21-23 NLT).

After reading this verse for the first time, I got so scared! If people that were casting out demons and performing miracles weren't "good enough" to enter the Kingdom of Heaven, then what chance would I have? Then it hit me. It's not about being good enough or deserving enough because none of us are. It has nothing to do with listing off all the things we did or didn't do in life to try and "negotiate" with God. The Bible says God doesn't want us to do something in His name to get into Heaven. He loves you more than that. He wants a relationship with you and for you to do things simply because you love Him, not with some ulterior motive. You don't have to be some perfect, righteous person to be with God after you die. It's about *relying on God's Grace instead of your good deeds and doing so purely out of love for Him.*

It doesn't matter what journey you want to take in life. Just do it with a heart of wanting to help more than yourself. Take your goals and use them to inspire yourself and others as followers of Christ. When I talk about doing BIG things in this book, I'm not just talking about grand gestures or fantastic accomplishments. I mean for you to pursue what you truly love and succeed *with the intent of serving God.* You can do this no matter where your goals take you. Do things not with the motive of trying to get into Heaven or because you feel obligated, but because you want to do God's will. I know I fell into this trap of thinking that volunteering or trying to memorize Bible verses would somehow make me more worthy. I was missing the point. It's not about us or our deeds. It's about God's mercy toward our sins and being able to do things purely out of love for Him and the people around us. That, in my opinion, is true success and is far more meaningful than any empty promises this world can offer.

Figuring Out What Matters to You

Unfortunately, the saying that you can't have your cake and eat it too can sometimes ring true. Sometimes having the perfect career AND a ton of money, AND lots of free time isn't always possible. Ranking how essential each item is to you is the next step in figuring out what YOU want. Write down a list of ten important things to you, with number one being the most important. Examples include faith, family, friends, money, a house, career, education. What's the key to making you happy? As an example, for me, having a job I'm happy in is more important than making a lot of money in that career. Whereas having cash in the bank is more important than owning a fancy vehicle. Your way of ranking things could look different from someone else. That's good! How high something is on the list should determine how important it is to you and help you to align your goals.

Your Bucket List

A bucket list is a list of all the things you want to do before you die. What's on your list tells a lot about you and is a great way to sum up the legacy you want to leave behind as well as what you want to accomplish. Try writing down one hundred things you want to try, do, own, visit, or experience before you die. It doesn't matter how seemingly small or big the things are as long as it's something YOU want to do. Do you want to visit the Eiffel Tower? Or hike the Appalachian Trail? How about eating alligator meat? Or go for a hot-air balloon ride? It's your life, so make sure all the things on the list are things YOU want to do.

God-Given Talents

I believe God has given each of us gifts to share with the world. Sometimes it can be frustrating if you don't know what they are yet. To figure out your talent, think about something you've always wanted to try or love to do. It could be an instrument, sport, or subject in school. The only way you'll figure out if you like it is if you give it a try. Don't worry if you end up hating it. At least that's one step closer to finding *your gift*. What is that one thing you love talking about or doing? You can see a person's eyes light up when they start sharing their passion or talents. Personally, it took me a while to find things I was genuinely passionate about doing. And your interests can change over time. Just keep looking until you feel something "click." It will take work to hone your talents, but the world will genuinely be better off if you do.

Your Legacy

What do you want to leave behind when you die? Your legacy is the impact you can have on the world. It could mean mentoring a youth group and helping teens find Christ or inventing a cure to cancer. Both have a huge impact on people's lives. Think about what you want to change in the world and how you're going to go about doing it. Your legacy doesn't have to be some big statement to the world where everyone will remember you. Even if you make a difference in a few people's lives, sometimes that's more than enough.

When I was younger, I met a girl who was always so sweet to me. She had a huge heart and would make me feel included, even though she was older. She might not remember this, but her kindness made a HUGE difference in my life, and it's something I still remember years later. We all have stories like that proving that seemingly small things DO matter. No matter what you go out and achieve in life, be the type of person who positively impacts others because people will remember.

The question is, what do you want them to remember about you?

DO BIG!

CHAPTER 2:

HOW TO ACHIEVE YOUR GOALS

*"People are not lazy. They
simply have impotent goals—
that is, goals that do not
inspire them."*
— Tony Robbins

Now that you have a better idea of what you want
to achieve, it's time to make it happen. For this
chapter, I encourage you to focus on one thing that
you've specifically always wanted to do, so by the
end of this book, you'll have the tools you need
to get there. It could be learning a language, starting a business, or getting your captain's license.
Whatever it is, DO BIG. Aim for the stars, and
you'll land on the moon. Set your expectations
high. Ever wonder why some people achieve big
things and others just don't? Part of the reason for

this is that the size of their dreams determines the size of their success. People that only think small will not accomplish big things simply because they're limiting themselves before they've even tried.

On the other hand, people who set high goals are far more likely to achieve them because they've set the bar higher for themselves. Don't be afraid of failure, only of selling yourself short. This whole book is about helping you go for the gold and stop underestimating yourself. *Think Big, and you will Do Big things.*

I had a friend who wanted to become a law clerk instead of a lawyer because she didn't think she was smart enough. I told her that if she aimed to become a lawyer, then worst case, she would become a clerk. But if she aimed for just becoming a clerk, then she'd never become a lawyer because she sold herself short. She is currently at the top of her class in Law School and soon to graduate. Whatever your goal is, you should never be asking yourself if it's too bold or ambitious. It always shocks me how much tenacity can come from people when they're put to the test. When I tested for my 1st-degree black belt in Taekwondo, I had worked for years, spending countless hours training every week. I would never have made it if I didn't believe that I could do it. That day of testing required six hours of continuous exercise, sparring with opponents and breaking wooden boards with my hands and feet. By the end of the testing, I was physically and mentally exhausted. My left foot was swollen to the size of a melon. But when it was over, I became the first girl and youngest black belt in the history of the martial arts school. By pushing myself further than I ever thought I could go, I proved to myself that I could accomplish what I set my mind to do. It took me years of intensive training in a martial art to realize I didn't need to doubt myself.

Hopefully, you won't have to go through that, because frankly, you wake up sore in the morning! Instead, by recognizing that you can do what you set your mind to, you can focus your energy on what you need to achieve. See the goal. And make that goal BIG. Perhaps it requires lots of push-ups and sweating to get to your destination. Maybe it's a series of mental hurdles you have to overcome. Either way, once you realize there is no limit to what you want to achieve, no one will be able to stop you from becoming even more successful in accomplishing all your goals.

How to set goals

It's important to set reasonable goals to guarantee you'll be successful in achieving what you want. First, think about something YOU have always wanted to accomplish. Make sure your goals are what you want to do and ask yourself why it's important to you. Don't do something just because someone else wants you to do it. If you aren't motivated, it'll be so much harder to achieve it. Instead, focus on goals you've set for yourself and are something you want. If your heart is in the right place, your head will be too.

Think Big

The key to being successful is to DO BIG things. To do that, you first have to Think Big. Take your goals and imagine ways you can make them more ambitious, more daring. Make sure you haven't shrunk your dreams down because you don't think you can do it. If you wanted to be a doctor and have now settled for becoming a nurse because you don't feel smart enough, you're not giving yourself a fair shot at succeeding.

There are already so many people out there who will try and tell you what you can and can't do. Being self-defeating is only adding to the noise.

Instead, focus on thinking Big, and not on the doubts of others. The worst thing that can happen is you fall short, and even if you do, you'll still be better off than if you didn't try in the first place. For me, instead of just becoming an Eagle Scout and working towards twenty-one merit badges, I decided to try earning them all. I never set out to become the first girl or to make some political statement. It was just something that looked fun to try and to see if I could achieve. The worst-case scenario was I would fall short of my goal, but if I hadn't tried, I would have *guaranteed* I'd never succeed. You WILL surprise yourself with what you're able to achieve if only you're willing to push yourself.

Embrace Failure.

Sound strange? If you live your life in fear of something, it will limit what you achieve. Being afraid of failure means you won't take the risks that you need to succeed. Anything worth doing isn't going to be easy, or everyone would have already done it. You must be the one to decide whether you'll be willing to take a risk and push yourself or let the fear of falling short affect your success. We'll talk about this more in Chapter eight.

Set a Time Limit.

The key to setting and achieving goals is setting a time limit to complete them. I don't know about you, but I'm a huge procrastinator, so by setting a time limit, I help myself stay focused on meeting my deadline. Instead of wording goals like "I want to graduate college," put precisely when you plan on achieving your goal, such as "I want to earn my master's degree before my twenty-fifth birthday."

Categorize Your Goals.

By grouping your goals as short or long-term, you can figure out what your next steps should be to achieve them. Short-term goals can take a day to a few months to complete. An example would be getting all 'A's' on your report card. Long-term goals can take a few years or more to earn. Examples would be getting elected as a member of Congress or saving up for a house. Long-term goals can be broken down into short-term goals to help you stay motivated and stick to what you want to achieve.

Break it Down.

Taking a long-term goal and then separating it into short-term goals is a great way to keep yourself motivated. For example, when I earned my black belt, my short-term goals were getting to the next belt every few months or every year. After several years, I eventually reached my long-term goal of becoming a black belt but having those short-term goals helped me stay motivated and to stick it out in the long term. The belt system in most martial arts is set up in this way. Setting short-term accomplishments that lead to the overall big picture. Map out steps you'll take daily, weekly, monthly, and yearly to get where you want to go. If my goal were to read the Bible from cover to cover in a year, I'd take the total number of pages and divide it by the number of days I would plan on reading it. That gives me the number I would need to read daily to get to my goal. All you have to do is commit to working towards your goal and staying motivated on what you want to achieve.

Be Specific.

Word your goal so you know exactly how you plan on getting there and when. Don't be generic and instead focus on defining what you want to accomplish. Instead of saying, "I want to get in shape," say, "This summer, I'm going to jog three miles every morning from 6:00 to 6:30 am." This will help you figure out what you need to do to get to your goals.

Make a Plan.

Even though it's not guaranteed you'll stick to it, having a plan is a great way to envision how to get where you want. You should answer basic questions such as how much time your goal will take, what your next steps are, and if it's short-term or long-term. Ask yourself how you'll stay motivated, how much money you'll need and why you're doing it. List important deadlines and put the list in a place where you'll see it daily to help you stay driven in sticking to the plan. If there is a better way to get to your goal, be willing to adapt and remember you're only able to control yourself, not those around you.

Research How to Get There.

It's essential to know the information you need to achieve your goals. For example, if you're trying to get into a particular college, study what they look for in applicants. Researching this beforehand will help you map out a plan and figure out the best way to manage your time.

Make a Vision Board.

Making a vision board is a great way to map out what you want your future to look like so you can focus on getting there. You can print out all sorts of important things and place them in a collage. Then, put it somewhere you'll see it on a day-to-day basis so you can work toward your goals. For me, I had a poster of all the merit badges for scouting hanging up in my room with little checks next to each one I had completed.

Manage Your Time Well.

One of the biggest mistakes people make when working on goals is doing tasks that aren't productive. For me, I'll work hard on something and then realize that if I just took a few seconds to ask myself if I needed to do it to get to my goal, the answer would have been no. Save yourself the headache of wasted time by questioning how a project benefits you before you start it.

Cut Out Distractions (Social Media).

To get to your goals, it's important to stay focused on the task at hand. This can be incredibly hard since there are so many distractions we have to put up with, from cell phone notifications to younger siblings, that it can feel impossible to get anything done. If you're like me and struggle with staying focused, there are plenty of methods to help. I've had to physically move my phone away from me while I work because the urge to check it is so tempting. Turning on 'Do Not Disturb' for specific hours during the day is also helpful. You can ask that your friends don't text you during certain times and limit how many times a day you check social media. While I work, I often wear fully soundproof headphones (we're talking construction level quality here), so I don't get distracted by my two siblings, phones ringing, or the neighbor's lawn mower. People we like can also be a big, *Ahem,* distraction, but there are ways to handle this as well. There's nothing wrong with losing focus from time to time when thinking about a crush or date, but when it becomes obsessive, that's never a good thing. Make separate plans to hang out instead of trying to "work" together on tasks.

Work Smart, Not Just Hard.

The funny thing about achieving your goals is that reality is often the opposite of what people think. We're always told to work hard for things, but I've found this not completely accurate. You can work hard at something every day, but if it's not getting you anywhere, then it's a waste of time. *Just because you're working hard at something doesn't mean it's helping you get to your goals.* That's why it's so important to work smart. Spend your time well and on tasks that will help you achieve your goals. Working smart just means looking at jobs beforehand to find the most effective way of completing them. I promise that doing this will save you so much unnecessary effort.

Try, Try, and Try Again.

The truth about achieving your goals is that you have to work for them and be willing to give up certain things. Getting to your dreams won't always be pretty and can mean a lot of grunt work to get there. But I've found that the more effort you put into something, often the more significant the reward. When working to earn all the merit badges, I would often sleep on the floor of a tent, study late into the night, then wake up before dawn to go to merit badge classes. For almost a year, I lived out of a 22-inch blue suitcase that I took to more than a dozen states and Scout camps across the country. Working hard for that goal could mean anything from hiking the Appalachian trail with a twenty-pound backpack to memorizing over a thousand worksheet answers. At many points, it took every ounce of strength I had to keep going.

Once, while camping in Georgia, my entire tent flooded from the heavy rain. Everything was soaked: my clothes, worksheets, even my cell phone. Instead of getting to curl up to sleep after going on a ten-mile hike through the wilderness, I spent hours mopping up the mess, starting a fire, and hanging everything out to dry. The next day, I woke up early and headed off to class, but I made sure to check the forecast this time.

Your goals will often push back. They should be a challenge to achieve because the whole point is to push yourself to do things you've never done before. To become the first girl in scouting to earn all the merit badges required a level of determination and discipline I didn't even know I possessed. A typical work week for me would mean either a long drive or flight while reading scouting workbooks and completing worksheets before I arrived at the campsite. Once there, I'd set up my tent and camp and then log on to an online merit badge class in the evenings with my filled-out worksheet and prerequisites completed. Depending on what time zone I was in, the course would often go late into the night. Then, it was usually a week-long camp with each day or several days at a time spent focused on a particular merit badge. I would learn to do everything from water skiing to archery to skeet shooting. Or nuclear science, archaeology, and electronics. During the weekend, sometimes, I'd be able to go home to Florida for a day or so to collect my other worksheets, work on prerequisites, and wash my laundry. I had to be in the best physical shape of my life and recall hundreds of pieces of information without mixing up class work. Although there were moments I wanted to quit, it was a reward in itself to go on all these adventures. That's the best part about working toward goals YOU want to achieve; they won't feel like work, and you'll surprise yourself with your ability to stay motivated. Working hard is just a part of achieving your goals. But when you work on something you love, you won't want to quit.

How to Achieve Your Goals

Getting to a goal will be a challenge. That's the whole point. It's up to you to be willing to put in the work to get there. Sometimes that could mean physically working on something like training for a marathon. Other times it could be a mental challenge, like memorizing information for a biology test. They both are difficult but use different muscles. When I work on my goals, I can quickly become obsessed with getting there. Often, I'll pull all-nighters where I'll work on writing one of my books, tweak my website, edit photos/videos, practice speeches, memorize flashcards, research opportunities, and even exercise in the middle of the night. People ask me what makes me get up and work so hard. I'm no different from you when it comes to being motivated. The "real secret" about achieving your goals is that you have to love working on them. You could never convince me to work hours on end without a break if I didn't love what I was doing. There are some areas in life where I'm a huge procrastinator and hate doing a particular task. When it comes to filling out forms or responding to text messages, I'm the worst! But, writing and motivational speaking are two things I've wanted to do ever since I was young, and I don't consider it work. The saying that, "If you find something you love, you won't ever have to work a day in your life," could not be more accurate. If you want to achieve your goals, you have to love what you do. Find that one thing that drives you and you will go far. Please don't waste your time with something you have no interest in because it will show.

Don't Let Anyone Push You Around.
People will not only try and push you around, but they'll also try to push you down. For some, the thought someone could be achieving something is perceived as a threat, and they feel the need to destroy your chances of succeeding. I've found in my personal experience that people who don't do this are rare. There are lots of critics. Lots of so-called 'trolls' looking to tear down your accomplishments. That's why it's so important not to roll over from pushback. This doesn't mean you ignore constructive criticism, just those looking to make you feel bad only for the sake of doing so. Take criticism as a way to motivate yourself to achieve your goals and prove your critics wrong. Whatever you do, don't let *their* doubts get in *your* head. Focus on what you need to accomplish and not on their negativity.

Balance Working Hard and Working Smart.
I see this a lot where people are willing to put the work in, but they spin because they don't plan. Or vice versa, where someone's spending all their

time planning and doesn't dig in and do what needs to be done. You have to be willing to do both. You can maintain a balance by trying to pull away occasionally with what you're working on and by considering other options.

No matter what, getting to your goals will be hard work. There will be people that help you and others who actively work against you. You might have to start over from scratch or adjust your expectations. Whatever challenges you come across, know they will shape you into a more experienced and stronger person. Even if you don't end up achieving exactly what you wanted, and your ending looks different than your initial vision, you'll have proven to yourself that you have what it takes to succeed.

CHAPTER 3:
THE SECRET TO MOTIVATION

*"It's hard to beat a person
who never gives up."*
—Babe Ruth

Once you know what your goals are and how to get there, the only thing you need to do now is to find a way to keep focused and stay motivated. Every person is different, but the more you learn about yourself, the easier it will be to keep yourself on track to accomplishing your goals. I'll cover how to figure out what distracts you, find solutions, and stay focused on effective reward strategies.

One of the things I'm most often asked is what makes me so motivated to achieve my goals. I found that being determined and staying focused isn't just something people wake up one day and have. Just like many other things, it's a skill that you have to work at developing. I've identified five "secrets" to motivation and focus that will help you on your way to achieve Big things.

The first secret is realizing that *anyone can learn how to stay motivated.* It's not something that only certain people can have. ANYONE can learn the art of motivating themselves and others. You just have to figure out what motivates you and find effective ways to use this to your advantage. It doesn't matter where your life has taken you or what you have or haven't achieved. What counts is your attitude and willingness to keep going even when you're ready to quit.

The second secret is that *motivation is something you have to keep working to achieve.* This can be hard because there are many days where you might feel like quitting, and staying motivated will feel impossible. That's where the real struggle begins. It's up to you to push yourself even when you don't feel like you have anything to keep you going. I would use small "rewards" for myself when feeling like I wanted to quit my goals. For example, I'd write 'To Do' lists for the day and title them "Stuff I GET to do today." Some of the items on the list would be cleaning my room, studying for an exam, doing laundry, and other things that no one in their right mind would look forward to doing. But by acting as though they were a reward after a day of working hard on my primary goals, it was a small way I could help myself to stay motivated, take a 'break' and still do all the things I needed to get done.

The third secret is *realizing that different things motivate different people.* For some, it is spending more quality time with their family or loved ones. For others, it is working toward independence or more money. This leads immediately to **the fourth secret**: *learning how to use what motivates people to the advantage of both parties.* Some of the most successful business people will tell you that the secret to getting others to help them was by being able to read people well enough to know what they want. Now, you might not have any employees just yet, but you can certainly still apply this to all sorts of areas in your life. If you need someone to help you, simply figure out what best motivates them. Once you can identify and understand how to motivate yourself and others, you will become successful in being able to work with others productively.

The key is figuring out what drives certain people and using it to help them perform the best they can. Some people find that earning **money** is what motivates them. If this is the case for you, you might prioritize a high-paying salary over a job you like doing. If money is an incentive, then try rewarding yourself with cash bonuses after achieving specific goals. For example, if you're trying to complete a 5k, reward yourself with putting $50 in your wallet to spend once you finish.

Money isn't the only motivator. Do you find that you work best when assignments have a **deadline**? Set times and dates to finish and stick to the timetable. If you naturally thrive in **competition**, working in aggressive environments with other people is a great way to stay motivated. Try sticking to sports, careers, and activities where you have to prove yourself against others. When people doubt you, do you feel determined to prove them wrong? If so, **opposition** is probably a way you feel motivated. You can thrust yourself into situations where people will likely challenge your views or reasoning so you can combat them and push them forward. If you work hard every day to try to get or keep a certain **lifestyle** (i.e., one with a big house, nice car, club membership), try motivating yourself to envision the life you want to have. You can create a vision board with all the luxuries you want and put it someplace where you'll see it each morning. When working on your goals, is it crucial people know your name and what you've accomplished? If **recognition** is what motivates you, make sure to take some time after achieving each goal to receive the attention you deserve for your achievements. You could have a party to celebrate once you've finished to help you stay motivated on goals in the future. When you think of success, does it look like having many loyal followers on social media or your picture on billboards? If **fame** is what you're after, focus on goals that will help you get there. Reward yourself with envisioning the attention you'll receive once you complete your goals. If you want to be at the top and oversee hundreds or thousands of employees, **control** could be your motivating factor. Prioritize working your way to the top of your field, and you may find yourself with the respect of your peers and have a lot of say in your career.

As cheesy as it sounds, **helping others** is one of the most significant motivating factors for me. I envision all the people I can impact with my work if I need help to stay motivated on a task. It's what helped me get up early in the morning to work on merit badges, knowing that each negative comment I received was one that a girl later on, hope-fully, wouldn't have to hear. Plus, it feels good to give back to others! If you relate to this one, try activities to see your impact on other people. You could reward yourself after achieving your goals by spending time volunteering at a place where you can make a difference.

The fifth secret is *learning to stay focused.* Some of my friends and I call ourselves (dramatic music) *The Modern Lost Generation* because, in a world full of temptations and distractions, it's easy to lose sight of what's important. Getting lost in a sea of content, influencers, and peer pressure has never been such a problem, but that's why follow-ing your path is more important than ever.

You and I make up this *modern lost generation.* Do you feel confused as to who you are? Worried about what lies ahead? Do you ask yourself if this is all there is to life? Are you concerned by the polar extremes of modern-day politics or about what's true and what part of the "truth" is being distorted for someone else's benefit? Maybe you're just trying to fit in or get more followers online to feel valued. Or looking to belong to a group, so you don't have to feel so alone anymore. Maybe you're doing trends not because you want to but because you want others to help make you feel valued. Perhaps you've given up and are at the point where you feel like you'll never be good enough or important enough to belong. It all seems so *lost*.

You aren't wrong for wanting or feeling any of this. Everyone, on some level, wants to be accepted and loved. And in reality, you aren't lost at all. You know what you want deep down. You just have to find yourself again.

Remember when you were little, and life was simpler? What did you want then? Was it to be famous on Tik Tok or get the hottest date to prom? Or was it something much more basic but boiled down into who you *really are*? So then, who are you? Not the bio on social media, what you tell your friends, or a list of adjectives or pronouns. There's more to you than that. Your impact on people is more than letters or words strung together. If you're looking to feel motivated in life, you must realize your value to others first. Once you see this, you'll understand you CAN make a difference. Your life has a purpose, but you must also give it meaning through your actions. Don't waste your time. Use it to help other people. Use it to show others love. Use it to rediscover yourself and find God.

<u>You aren't lost</u>. You just need to find your path again. Distractions are the things in life that will try and pull you away from your goals. This could be anything from social media to gossip, but its effects are the same. They can cause you to lose sight of your goals and the person you want to become. To stay motivated, you must figure out what distracts you most and develop reasonable ways to avoid it from happening. Below are some common distractions we all face and ways we can work to put them in their place to do BIG things.

Phones & Electronics

In all of human history, it's never been easier to delay assignments and procrastinate. Our generation possibly has it worse than any when focusing because of all the technological advancements over the last few decades. But this is something you've probably already found out for yourself.

Most of my childhood was unique in that I thought Apple was a type of fruit. My mom had a flip phone until I was thirteen, and I wasn't really around people who played video games. It sounds crazy, but I'm thankful I got to grow up away from all the technology that other people my age were exposed to, and it's sad to think that lifestyle is becoming rarer by the day. Even my siblings and I had very different childhoods despite just being a few years apart from each other. When I was younger, hanging out with friends meant going fishing or playing in the park. Now, a lot of the time, it can look like playing video games with people you may never meet in real life. For a person to not be on their cell phone now is considered almost unusual. My family and I were often in airports while traveling, and we were usually sitting in the terminal reading books. Many people—all over the globe—approached us and commented how unusual it was to see a family sitting all together reading.

In just a few short years, a lot about growing up has changed. Just because things are different doesn't make it wrong or bad. Without a doubt, technology has the potential of saving lives and making our lives more enjoyable, but only if we use it for those purposes. The problem is that a lot of people (myself included) have used technology as a way to escape our reality instead of working to fix the one we're living. Whatever you're running away from, whether it's a broken relationship or the nasty words of someone at school, there is a better way to deal with it. It's easy to fall into the trap of thinking that a phone will distract us from our problems when it usually ends up creating more.

Be honest with yourself. If technology is something you struggle with as a distraction (whether from apps, video games, social media, or the Internet), stop letting yourself get sucked into it all. You're the only person who has enough willpower to control yourself and form healthy habits instead. The scary part is that for someone who did not grow up with anywhere near the exposure kids are getting from technology now, I still struggle with the temptation to want to use my device all the time. I can only imagine how hard it would be for kids who have been indoctrinated into that technology from such a young age.

It took me a long time to even recognize that technology could be a form of addiction because I usually imagine smoking, drinking, or drugs when I think about unhealthy habits. **But anything you can't say no to is an addiction.** Ask yourself when you're on a device if you'd be able to put it down right then and there for a few weeks without constantly thinking about how many likes a post received, who's texting you, or if your inbox has new emails. It's not your fault if you'd find yourself struggling. The cards have been unfairly stacked against you from the beginning since the apps are designed to be as addicting as possible.

So why should we bother trying to disconnect in the first place? Anything that has that much control in our lives is never a good thing. We need to take back the reigns and stop letting distractions get in the way of our goals.

According to the Douglas Mental Health University Institute, "the average young person will have spent some *ten-thousand* hours gaming by the time they are 21." Ten-thousand hours? Imagine what you could do with that time. It takes a person roughly 500-hours to reach basic fluency in a language like French or Spanish. How many languages could you learn? With that time, you could earn a bachelor's degree or get licensed as a commercial airline pilot three times over. By just managing our time better, we can accomplish so much more. Video games and technology have a place in our lives, but how big a place is up to you. A mentor of mine said not to "waste time-saving fantasy worlds when the real world is on fire."

Imagine the difference we could make in ourselves, our communities, and our country if we all just spent less time on our devices. We could change the world instead of just our profiles. What if we strive to make living in the real world better than the fake one? If your reality were better than the one online, you probably wouldn't even waste time posting about it because you'd be too busy having fun.

Go on adventures and find people who will tag along without getting on their phones the whole time. **Make a conscious effort to leave your devices behind**. I try to avoid taking my phone to places like church or the grocery, so I'm not tempted to get on it. You can also try leaving your devices at home during longer stints, like hanging out with friends or on vacation. **Find out your excuses and come up with solutions.** For me, I'd always cite "listening to music" as an excuse to get on my phone. I found that instead of just listening to music, I'd constantly be checking notifications instead. My solution was to download songs onto my old iPod and use that instead so I wouldn't feel the urge to check my phone anymore.

Set the expectation that you won't always reply to messages right away, so you don't feel pressure. I'm the worst at responding to texts and emails, but at least everyone knows this and doesn't have the expectation that I'll answer anytime soon. Anyone who demands you respond right away (apart from making sure you're OK) is not considerate of your own life or time.

Meet up with people in the real world. This is honestly one of the best ways I've found to take a break from electronics. Instead of sitting in a room playing video games together with friends and family, go kayaking or to the beach, or take a simple walk together. Find people willing to go out and do things and who won't be on their phones the whole time.   Even then, many people don't disconnect. Once, I went to the beach with my friends. We were all playing football, tossing frisbees, and chasing each other in the water. We had a blast when a group of women walked up to us. At first, I thought they would scold us for being too loud, but they said it made their day to see us having fun together, so much so that they pointed out how rare it was to see even at the beach. I looked around and saw people sunbathing while on their phones and realized we were the only ones in the water. It was just like the people I'd seen waiting for a plane in the airport, except this time, there was a bright blue ocean out there waiting for them.

The best part about being with a group of people who aren't on their phones is that they live in *real life* and will go and do things with you. I get how tempting it is to get on devices because I'm in the same boat myself. Our whole generation and the ones who come after us will have to deal with this, perhaps to an even greater extent. But, maybe if we're able to face it together and prioritize the real world, we can not only get better ourselves but improve what's around us as well.

If you're stuck in a reality you hate, don't try and find a new one. Fix the one you're already in, and you won't feel like you have to escape as often. I had a friend who would play video games whenever his abusive father was around to distract himself from his current situation. But instead of physically leaving or getting help, he would spend his time sitting in a chair. Finally, he decided to unplug the gaming console permanently and do everything he could to turn his life around. I remember him telling me that although he may have won in the video games, he had almost lost in the real world because he let the abuse control his life and decisions. Now he's been able to improve himself and build up a better world that he doesn't have to log out of anymore. Phones and tech can be our biggest distractions, but only if we give them the control to do so. By taking a step back and working on our goals in the real world, we can make a lasting difference for ourselves and the people around us. The more you invest in the real world, the better living in it will be.

Social Media

Social media may be an even more significant threat. It has its pros and cons, but that doesn't stop it from being a distraction if we let it affect us too much. It has the potential to be a fantastic resource to connect with friends, customers and sell products. But, just like almost anything else in excess, it can quickly become all-consuming and obsessive because *that's what it is designed to do*.

I have had to put my phone in another room with the notifications off so I don't get distracted while working. It's scary to think my willpower is tested so much by a bunch of pixels on a screen. I'm not saying you shouldn't go on social media. Just try to do so a reasonable amount of time per day. And if you're like me, where you pick up your phone to respond to a comment only to find yourself scrolling through Girlyzar memes twenty minutes later, then I would recommend removing your phone from sight when working. This is one of the hardest things for me because I didn't even recognize it had become a problem. I saw a lot of people my age spending hours on their phones every day. But **just because something is normal doesn't mean it's healthy**.

The biggest problem I've found with social media is not necessarily the time you spend, but that it makes us constantly feel the need to compare ourselves to others. It makes it that much harder to feel good about ourselves, move on from relationships, and be content with what we already have. Don't let social media become a distraction for you. Fight back against its addictive nature. **Mentally distance yourself from the apps** and focus on **building relationships with people in the real world**. If possible, **limit how much you share and post about your life** and try **taking weeklong (or longer) breaks**. Sometimes when I take breaks from social media, I'll lose hundreds of followers on Instagram at a time, which is why I can't tie my worth to it. You shouldn't either. If you feel yourself getting sucked into scrolling through endless content, try to **recognize when and why you're doing this**. Are you bored, stressed out, upset, or even hungry? Address those issues instead of trying to distract yourself. I found that I'd usually go on my phone right before bed, so I began plugging my phone in on the opposite side of my room to make sure I wouldn't feel the need to check it anymore. I promise you'll set yourself apart when you're willing to recognize how addictive it is and work to prevent it from affecting your life and your goals.

Gossip and Rumors

Possibly the most upsetting and distracting topic on this list is the spreading of rumors. We've all been burned by someone's words. I've had my fair share of rumors and stories about me, and I know how painful it is to be betrayed by a friend. It can distract you from your goals because it's not like you can just move your phone into another room for the problem to go away. The whispers continue regardless.

You might have to face the rumor every day at school, endure it at church, or get nasty texts from people who believe it. I had so-called friends who would go around behind my back, saying I was in-volved with someone just to try and embarrass me. The worst part wasn't the betrayal but the conse-quences their words had on my 'friendships' with other people. The experience was enlightening be-cause there was a separation between the people who believed the rumor and those who believed me. Luckily, I was able to see who my true friends were and discovered how quickly others had turned on me. It was a struggle not to let the gossip affect me, but thankfully I found I could manage it. The good news is you can too.

There will always be people in life who will try and tear you down, which is why you have to be stronger than the storm. Don't let the idle gossip of others get inside your head and stop you from achieving your goals. Spend time with people who have your best interests in mind and won't betray you. Don't hang around with people who gossip about others because chances are they're doing the same thing to you. Be selective about who you trust and reveal things to, and, most importantly, don't let the gossip affect your decision-making.

The rumor about me involved one of my friends. At first, I thought maybe if I avoided him, the rumor would die down, and everyone would move on. But I realized that by ignoring my friend, I let the people spreading the story know that they had hurt me. I decided that completely ignoring the gossip and going about my life was the best thing I could do. Not only did it show that I didn't care, but I was also able to discover my true friends in the process.

If what's happening is harming your reputation and isn't true, you can confront the gossipers directly. Don't be afraid to stand your ground and prove your point. If they're remorseful, they'll want to undo the damage they've caused by apologizing and clarifying their mistake with others. If not, they may continue, but don't let that stop you from trying to fix the issue. At some point, you can't control every aspect of what people think of you. You CAN continue to be your strong, confident self and not worry about the jealousy of others. Set your sights on higher goals than the rumor spreading of unhappy people and pray that they find more profound things to do with their lives and time.

Hunger and Sleep Deprivation

As essential as sleep and food seem, they're easy to forget about and brush aside. When working on my goals, I would sometimes go all day just eating a granola bar or an apple and only get a few hours of sleep at night. But over time, these two became tremendous obstacles and made it harder to achieve my goals in the long run. The longer I pushed aside basic needs, the harder it became to concentrate and find enough energy to get everything done. I finally decided I was going to prioritize getting enough sleep and eating enough food. Almost immediately, I was able to concentrate better and accomplish much more.

If you're a workaholic like me, taking breaks can make you feel guilty. Finding a healthier balance will make it easier to achieve your goals and live a more balanced lifestyle. Try setting alarms and pulling away for a few minutes to grab a snack or even take a catnap. Or, at the very least, add some variety. You don't have to stop being productive. Just switch it up a little. For example, during a typical day, I might study for an exam, do my laundry, work on my book, go to the gym, edit photos, and rehearse for an upcoming speech. By shifting between each task, I can get a lot done while also staying focused for a more extended amount of time. If you have a lot of homework assignments, rotate between each until you're finished, and don't feel bad about taking breaks. If you're starting to lose focus more and more, it's your brain trying to tell you it needs a break.

When You're Ready to Quit

Call it burnout, procrastination, or a breakdown, but we all get to that point in life when we're ready to quit. It can be so tough after working hard at something to keep going. Maybe something happened that caused you to lose faith in your goal, or you have to start over from scratch. Perhaps, you have to decide if your goal is worth continuing to pursue. I know I got to the point where I was physically and emotionally drained for my black belt testing. I had to break ten wooden boards in a row. I was already exhausted, and I only had one board left. My knuckles were raw. I was utterly drained, and no matter how hard I punched, the last board wouldn't break. I had two choices. Either I could give up and go home without the belt, or I could keep going even though it hurt. I realized that I had worked for years to get to this point, and to throw all that hard work away wasn't worth it. I was familiar with pain and knew that pushing myself just a bit further would be worth it in the end. I paused and slammed my fist into the board one last time. It splintered into pieces. My knuckles were bruised and bloody, but I had achieved what I set out to do. To persevere taught me that any goal worth reaching would be hard to achieve. It's when you keep going and succeed that makes it worth all your hard work.

I understand feeling like you're ready to give up. I can't tell you how many times in my life I've been ready to throw the towel in and quit. But whenever I feel that way, I force myself to look ahead. Think about how far you've come and all the work you've put in to get yourself to where you are now. If you're feeling burnt out, take a break. I find that even going for a walk or spending time in nature is enough to get me back on track. Sometimes, a much-needed break to just step back and look at the big picture is what we need to see our next steps.

Burnout

Sometimes quitting is just a form of burnout—that feeling we get when we've been stressed about something to the point that it causes mental/physical exhaustion. When I feel this way, I usually ask myself rhetorical questions like, 'What's the point?' and come up with other melodramatic excuses that avoid getting the work done. Sometimes, when we feel like quitting, it's just time to do what needs to be done to alleviate the stress.

While finishing my first two years of college when I was fourteen, I had to pass a challenging biology course. Studying for it was time-consuming and mentally draining, but I didn't have the option of taking many breaks if I wanted to move on to the next class. Whenever I would find my mind wandering off or feeling ready to quit, I'd imagine all the pressure taken off my shoulders once I finished the class. I threw myself into studying and working for hours to learn and memorize everything I needed. For me, I find that just "digging in" is a great way to finish what needs to be done.

Another great way to avoid burnout is by surrounding yourself with ambitious people who will help motivate you. Just being around others who are focused and healthy can sometimes be enough to encourage you to keep doing the same. If you're having trouble finding people like this, it could be that you're looking in the wrong places. I've found that some of the most driven people are busy on their own goals and not usually caught up in gossip, posting on social media (unless building a brand or a business), or just hanging out around town. They're the ones taking the initiative to work on their own goals without anyone having to tell them twice. You'll find people like this with similar interests the more you work on your own goals.

Procrastination

Procrastination is something we all do, but you have to put the work in and get the job done to accomplish big things. Sometimes you have to "bite the bullet" to get where you need to go. Luckily, this is something you can teach yourself and improve upon every day. The better you are at preventing yourself from procrastinating, the easier it will be to achieve your goals. One of the ways I avoid putting things off is by putting my anxiety in its place. I find that we most often procrastinate when we're nervous or worried about the task ahead. By finding ways to cope with stress, we can stop delaying what needs to get done once and for all.

As we wrap up this chapter, remember the five secrets to motivation:

1. Realize that anyone can learn how to stay motivated.
2. Motivation is something you have to keep working at to maintain.
3. Recognize that different things motivate different people.
4. Learn how to use what motivates people to the advantage of both parties.

5. Don't get distracted. Staying focused and motivated on tasks is a skill we can all hone.

Once you understand your motivators, you'll be on the right track to accomplishing everything you set out to do. And if you're able to persevere and stay motivated, you will achieve your goals.

DO BIG!

CHAPTER 4:

HANDLING OPPOSITION

"Show me someone who has done something worthwhile, and I'll show you someone who has overcome adversity."
—Lou Holtz

Learning to manage opposition is one of the most important things you'll need to know to get to your goals. But it's also something that almost everyone struggles to do. Opposition can be an internal or external force trying to push you down and make you feel bad about yourself. We have all met people who thrive on destroying the confidence and sense of self-worth in those around them. Or maybe you struggle with a voice inside your head telling you that no matter what you've achieved, you will never be enough. Whatever these internal or external voices are telling you, it's time to permanently flick the off switch because IT DOESN'T MATTER WHAT THEY THINK. You are the only one who can truly determine what you want and what's best for you.

This chapter will help you stop caring about what all the negative voices in your life have to say and help you handle prejudice, self-doubt and build unshakable confidence. Sound great? Having a core that isn't affected by internal or external doubt is one of the most potent ways to achieve your goals and set yourself apart from the majority. The truth is that many people struggle with not feeling good/attractive/smart enough, and it gets in the way of their goals. I've seen so many people already shortchange themselves because they don't believe in themselves and don't bother trying. They let the negative voices in their life impact their decisions to the point where they give up without even putting up much of a fight. In this chapter, you will learn how to battle opposition and use it to motivate you. Let's get started!

External Opposition

No matter what you do in the modern world, chances are you'll run into someone, somewhere, criticizing your decisions. The internet makes it easy to ridicule others and that much harder to tune it all out. Now it's not just politicians but private citizens who are faced with their choices being mocked or scolded. It can feel like you're drowning in a sea of people trying to become something impossible to obtain, but I've realized that YOU are too good for it all. You deserve to feel happy and not have others belittle or make you feel small. Sit back and think about how hypocritical comments and posts on the internet can be, and you might start laughing.

When you look at all the images of people on social media, just imagine each of them adding filters, adjusting their waist size, and taking hundreds of pics to get the "perfect" one to post. We've created our own monsters, and now we're paying the price. Scrolling through everyone's photoshopped lives online, you have to realize that what they're presenting to the world isn't real, only what they want you to see. So naturally, most of the content is an ideal that just doesn't exist. You and I know this already, but it still doesn't change that it's hard to feel good about ourselves when we're constantly bombarded with all the things we can't have. We all have something we wish we could change about ourselves, whether it's our hair color, oily skin, or how many zeros are at the end of our paycheck. We want to be accepted and loved by our culture and the people around us. The only problem with this is that what society has presented as an ideal just doesn't exist.

The only way to beat the cycle is by not letting a bunch of fake images and haters determine your self-worth. You are already beautiful, handsome, and precisely the way God made you. You don't need to change anything about yourself because you are already perfect and loved for who you are. Once you finally come to this conclusion, you won't have to worry anymore about chasing after becoming something you're not in the hopes of finally feeling accepted. You need to be the one to accept yourself first, and then others will see you for who you are too. You're just as important as any supermodel or celebrity, and God views you both equally. It doesn't matter to Him what you look like because He's able to look past all the superficialness and see you for the fantastic person you *really* are.

Sometimes, external opposition can look like people refusing to help you because they don't have faith in you. It's frustrating to have someone in your life who doesn't support your decisions and may try to become an obstacle on your path. Everyone's allowed their opinions, but if it's getting in the way of your goals, it's a problem you now have to fight to overcome.

On my journey to a hundred and thirty-seven merit badges, I faced many challenges in and out of my control. There were skills I had to master, knowledge I had to acquire, and tasks I needed to persevere through. I remember one time I handed in a twenty-page worksheet to my counselor that took days to complete. He glanced at it, then tossed it in the back of his truck and went to grab lunch. The next day he handed the papers back to me soaking wet with a smirk and said he wouldn't sign me off on the merit badge because he couldn't read my now smeared handwriting. I was so angry and ready to quit, but I had worked so hard to get to that point. I calmly took my dripping wet worksheet back to my tent.

Suddenly I realized I had taken pictures of each page before handing it to him as a backup. After all, one of the most important lessons the Scouts taught me was to always *be prepared*. The next day I returned to the man and handed him a newly printed copy of my merit badge worksheet, a pen, and my blue card so he could approve my work. After analyzing my papers, he finally signed off, got in his truck, and drove away. It's important to note that most people were overwhelmingly support-ive along my journey despite the ones who were not. It's up to YOU to decide at the end of the day whether you're going to focus on the good or the bad that you will face with your goals. It's not that you shouldn't acknowledge opposition, just that you shouldn't let it consume you. In my case, if I hadn't tried again, I might never have earned all the merit badges. Having obstacles is just a part of life, but how you deal with them determines your suc-cess. There will always be people in life who will try and push you down or make it harder for you to achieve your goals. It's up to you to take peoples' opposition and use it as motivation to succeed.

There were those along my journey who were against *girls* joining the *Boy* Scouts. And that's OK! Girls have been a part of Scouting since the beginning of the program (they just weren't able to earn the merit badges). When girls finally could do this, there was the perception that girls would have an easier path. I remember being in Georgia and listening to a kid gleefully explaining to a group of boys how he had "snuck a peek at a girl's hand-book." He said he knew "for a fact, it was easier than the boys, and that's why all the girls earn more merit badges than us!" I could have argued that wasn't true, but I decided to move on with my life and head to my next merit badge class. You can't let what other people say negatively affect you. Instead, let it roll off your back by laughing as you move on to more productive things. Whatever opposition you have to deal with right now, I challenge you to look at the bigger picture in life instead.

Internal Opposition

On the flip side, internal opposition is when you let all the outside voices get in your head. This can be incredibly harmful when working toward your goals because it's self-defeating and hard to eliminate. After a while, even people with great self-esteem can struggle with internal opposition because it tends to be the loudest and hardest voice to ignore.

I had a friend in my inner circle say some negative things about me. Even though they immediately apologized, and we both knew they didn't mean it, it still hurt. I started doubting myself, and it was like the floodgates of negativity had opened. Thankfully, I quickly realized I had almost let self-doubt win by giving it a voice. You have to be stronger than the negativity around you, or it will find a way in and try to destroy your confidence. This is one of the biggest problems I see our generation facing because of the amount of criticism we have to deal with daily. It's up to you to decide what voices you're going to listen to and which you choose to ignore.

Not Feeling Like You're Enough

Whatever it is you feel like you lack in your life, whether it's your level of fitness, intelligence, or your looks—know for a fact you are already MORE THAN ENOUGH. I've personally found that not feeling good enough stems from feeling as though you do not deserve love or that you're not receiving love in the right way. _You don't need to prove to anyone that you deserve love because that's already something you have_. You don't need to chase after a crush or lose weight or be someone you're not to get love. You already have unconditional love from God. Hopefully, you also have people in your life who love you for the amazing person you already are. And if you don't feel like you do, it's not because you're unworthy. It's because those people have fallen short of giving you the love you deserve.

Not feeling good enough about yourself can make you think you don't deserve love and can cause you to lower your self-worth. This is often apparent in the people we choose to date. Sometimes, we'll go out with people who aren't healthy for us because we think that's what we "deserve" or the best we can get. *Don't settle for what you think you deserve. Settle for what you know you want.* No matter what, know that you are already more than enough. You deserve nothing less than for people to treat you well.

Internal opposition is one of the most inhibiting factors you will face on the road to achieving your goals, so it's essential to know how to combat and shut down negativity. I've found that by not caring what people think, building self-confidence, and by standing up for yourself, you can shut down internal and external opposition for good.

Guarding Your Heart

Getting to the point in your life where you only let a few key people's opinions affect you is one of the most important lessons I've learned. I can't let random people have any real say in my life, or it would be devastating. When I became the first girl to earn all the merit badges in Scouts BSA, I received thousands of comments from people I had never met saying things like, "The world needs babymakers too, so you will always have a job." or calling me names like "nerd" and "freak." Honestly, most of the comments were downright hilarious, but if I had let a bunch of nameless profiles on the internet determine my self-worth, it would have been soul-crushing. This is why it's so important to distance yourself from outside people's opinions. It's a way to protect what truly matters.

My friends and family jokingly call me "The Onion" because of the many layers I have before I trust people. By being selective with who I trust and am close with, I can make sure they genuinely have my best interests in mind beforehand. The people I do let into my small inner circle have a significant impact on my life, and what they say matters a lot. I remain incredibly loyal to friends and family who have gained my trust and have proven themselves to have my best interests in mind time and time again.

Trust is one of the greatest gifts you can give to someone, and it's essential to make sure people earn it. I'm not saying you shouldn't be open with people, just that you're selective with who you trust until you know their intent. Think of some people you're able to trust and rely on and try giving them more of a voice in your life while reducing the volume from others. Don't let people who don't know the real you judge how you see yourself. Who are they to determine what you think? Instead of seeking external approval, focus on feeling confident in yourself first. Truly confident people don't need external approval to know they're already more than enough.

How to Stop Caring What the Negative Voices in Your Life Think

Sometimes it can feel like everyone's trying to pull you in different directions. This can be useful as we test out new ideas and figure out what we believe, but when outside influences become harmful, it's time to reevaluate how much we let them affect us. Most people have felt the hurt of others saying nasty things about them, myself included, but even though it might feel like the end of the world, you were destined for so much more than having to deal with such negativity. That doesn't take away the hurt of someone's cruel words or actions, but it can stop you from caring so much about what they think.

There will always be someone trying to make you feel bad about what you've accomplished. It's important not to let their negativity get in your head and instead focus on becoming the best person you can be despite their unhappiness. The first step in doing this is to find out where your self-doubt originates. Sit back and think about why you question yourself. Does it come from a specific person or group? I've found that people with self-defeating thoughts have often had someone in their lives cause them to not feel good enough through their words or actions. Almost everyone feels like a failure at some point in life, but this is only made worse by negative people looking to push you down. It would help if you found the people who are causing you to doubt yourself and distance yourself from them physically and emotionally. Remember, there will always be haters, but determining how you let it affect you is what matters, not what they're saying.

Building Confidence

This is one of the most remarkable ways you can combat negativity and become a leader. To boost your confidence, you have to believe in yourself. (Who knew that cheesy cat poster was so accurate?) Believing in yourself means trusting that you can achieve your goals. The best part about confidence is that it comes from the inside, so no one can take it from you no matter how hard they try.

You can boost your confidence by looking in the mirror (as corny as it sounds) and writing down a list of all the things you love about yourself. Instead of focusing on all the things you wish you could change, look at all the beautiful and unique traits God has given you. Try saying those positive attributes to yourself each morning as you get ready for the day ahead. Emphasize the best of you and dress to impress. When you go places, focus on presenting yourself in the best way possible. This doesn't mean wearing a ton of makeup and expensive clothes, but it does mean putting your best foot forward so you feel comfortable with who you are. Wear outfits that you feel confident in, and the feeling will emanate.

Focus on learning more about yourself, as we talked about in Chapter One. Knowing where you stand on issues and what you want not only helps boost inner confidence but shows others you are prepared and sure of yourself. Don't shrink back in the corner of the room. Stand tall. Speak up if you know the answers to questions and be willing to take constructive criticism and back up your responses.

Be kind to others. Whenever I see people being nasty, I can't help but think they must not be feeling good about themselves. In contrast, the most obvious sign that someone is confident is when they can be genuinely nice to others without feeling threatened.

Ever since I was little, my dad always told me that I could learn something from everyone. Even if what they're saying doesn't seem particularly useful at the moment, each person on this earth has something to offer. **Be willing to learn from others,** and you'll not only show you're confident in yourself but wise as well. **Don't shoot ideas down** just because they're not in line with what you think. Be open to listening to both sides of a story, and don't skip to conclusions. This will help you make better decisions and show you're confident enough in what you believe not to feel the need to drown out other people's opinions.

Admit mistakes in judgment when needed. No one's perfect, and by recognizing your flaws, you will come across as being aware instead of arrogant. One of the most significant signs I've found when someone is confident is when they can **laugh at themselves**. Everyone makes silly mistakes from time to time but being able to laugh it off instead of getting angry shows they are emotionally mature.

Focus on **being positive**. Be the person who looks on the bright side, and people will naturally be drawn to you just based on your attitude towards life.

Finally, actively work on your goals. Focus on what you want to achieve and reward yourself when you do. Feeling good about yourself is contagious, and people will take note when you carry yourself like the accomplished person you already are.

There is a difference between confidence and arrogance. It's so easy to mistake one for the other because you have to get to know a person before understanding the reasons for their behavior. A confident person believes in themselves and doesn't feel the need to make others feel bad. They usually have a positive outlook on life and like being around people. They give compliments freely and have a high set of morals. Confident people take responsibility when they make a mistake and accept other people for their differences. They can laugh at themselves and take risks because they're sure of their abilities.

On the other hand, an arrogant person usually speaks poorly about other people and will often push others down. They typically aren't trusting of people and are willing to bend the rules to get their way. They would rather make fun of others than themselves and can be very judgmental. Arrogant people usually struggle to make decisions and will do what feels good instead of what's right.

Stick Up for Yourself and Others

Not caring what people think doesn't mean you let them push you around or get away with it. If anything, you should stand up for yourself if what they're saying becomes harmful for yourself or others. Because as much as we try, at some point, negativity can take its toll. Remember that being passive isn't the same as not caring. If what they're saying doesn't remotely matter and you're able to tune it out, that's awesome! But if it starts to feel overwhelming, it's important to recognize and handle the problem. You can stand up for yourself by being deliberate and persistent in what you want to be changed. Don't accept when people are rude or nasty. You deserve to be treated with respect and kindness, so don't tolerate anything less.

It's also vital to pick your battles, so knowing when you should stand up for yourself is a great skill to have. If what someone is saying doesn't affect you, then don't worry about it. For example, I didn't respond to the comments online because it didn't matter what random profiles on the internet thought of me. There will always be people looking to start a fight. As long as they don't bother you, don't waste your time. But if what someone is saying isn't true affects your self-image, and most importantly, is upsetting for you, you need to stick up for yourself.

How to Stand Up for Yourself

Depending on the issue, this can be pretty simple or a bit complicated. Remember, if you're likely to be abused, you need to remove yourself from the situation and immediately get help. I talk more about how to escape from abusive relationships in Chapter Seven.

If the problem isn't likely to become too volatile, you need to confront them politely. Do not approach them when they're around other people. You likely won't have their full attention, or they may want to show off in front of their friends. Ask to talk one on one and speak in a respectful tone. Try not to sound too accusatory, as there is always the possibility it's a misunderstanding. Communicate what they've said or done that bothers you. If it's obvious they're not planning on changing their behavior, bring in a teacher/parent/guardian who you can count on to help. There's safety in numbers, so make sure to stick with people who have your back when others are nasty. If you both come to a resolution, make sure that all issues have been addressed and you have open communication in the future.

Please remember that any behavior that makes you feel uncomfortable is WRONG. While working towards one of my goals, I had a teacher suddenly touch my shoulders and whisper things in my ear. It made me feel very uncomfortable, and I immediately backed away. I knew I had to stand up for myself, even if it meant I didn't complete the class because I wouldn't want another person to be put in the same situation. Behavior that makes you feel uncomfortable is wrong no matter what, and it's up to us to recognize and stand up for ourselves and others. If you ever find yourself in a similar situation, speak up so the problem can be fixed. Especially if it's an adult or someone in a position of power over you, it can feel like nothing you do or say will change anything, or you might feel frightened to speak up. Know that what they're doing is wrong, and you have every right to tell them. It's better to stick up for yourself now than wishing you had later. Stand up for what you know is right.

How to Stick Up for Yourself Online

It's important to distance yourself from what's going on mentally in order to stand up for yourself in an online forum. The internet can be especially dangerous because instead of face-to-face interactions, some people feel they can say whatever they want without seeing the consequences. The people behind your screen don't get the privilege of knowing what a fantastic person you are because many times, they've never even met you in real life! And you don't know their whole story either, so try to have empathy for them. If what people are saying doesn't dramatically affect other people's opinions of you or your self-esteem, then don't waste your time firing back comments. That's what they want you to do. If it does start to affect you, involve a friend, family member, or guardian willing to help. Do not respond to the person because engaging them may just cause them to fire back. Instead, you can beat them at their own game by deleting their comments, unfollowing, flagging, reporting, or blocking them.

How to Stand Up for Others

Standing up for others is a great way to help people, boost your confidence, and sometimes even make a new friend. Plus, treating others the way you want to be treated is rewarding in itself. You can do this by not tolerating when people talk poorly about others behind their back.

I was in a group of friends when one of the girls started talking about how "high" this guy acted because of his "mental condition." I had never met the guy, but I was disappointed she would talk this way about anyone, so I discretely left. Many of my friends followed, which shows me I'm not alone in my disdain when people speak poorly about others. Not only that, but several months later, I unknowingly met the guy she was talking about, and we've been great friends ever since. It's funny sometimes how God works to bring people together to show that He sees us even when it feels like no one's watching.

To stand up for others, you have to be assertive and determined. Don't let the person push you around or tolerate the behavior. It can be scary to stick up for others, especially because you can become the new target. Most of the time, though, it just takes one brave person not to tolerate the behavior before they stop.

There are many ways you can stick up for people without aggressively getting in someone's face. Don't stand for gossip, spread rumors, and walk away from negative conversations. When people notice you doing these things, they will respect you. No one wants to be around negative or gossipy people because chances are, they'll do the same thing to you. Become the friend everyone wants to have by rising above the noise and sticking up for yourself and others.

Types of Opposition

Opposition is anyone or anything that looks to get in the way of your success. Opposition can be an unhealthy mindset, individual, or habit that's causing you harm instead of helping you get to your goals. I'll go over some main types: discrimination, negative body image, depression, drugs, smoking, alcohol use, and bullying, and how to combat each.

Discrimination

My whole life, I've done sports and activities that are typically male-dominated, such as Taekwondo, sailing, piloting, SCUBA diving, and Scouts BSA. I didn't participate in these to prove a point or try and infringe upon "letting boys be boys." I did them because they just seemed like fun. For the most part, I faced very little pushback and met many supportive people, but some were not always as encouraging. Sometimes people's own preconceived opinions and anger towards others prevent them from seeing clearly. The one thing I've learned from my experiences is that you shouldn't let other people's opinions deter you from success. Keep going, and you will eventually succeed, and people can either help you or move out of your way. Remember that anything worth doing won't be easy and that once you achieve your goals, no one can take what you've accomplished away from you. The worst they can do is make it harder to get where you're going—but if you don't give up, all they'll be is another hurdle you were able to overcome on your road to success.

Negative Body Image

As a teenage girl, this is something I struggle with, along with many of my friends. I once knew a stunningly beautiful girl. It was hard to believe someone that "perfect" could exist! What struck me as odd was the girl didn't see herself that way at all. She would say she needed to lose more weight, how she wasn't proportionate, or how her eyes were too close. I never once had noticed any of these "flaws." I thought it was disturbing that someone so beautiful could think of themselves as being "ugly."

That's the scary reality of having a negative body image. I can only imagine how many people look at themselves and don't see what everyone else does. Many girls, in particular, feel the pressure of looking a certain way to fit in. Have you ever just stared at yourself in the mirror and looked at all the things you wish you could change about yourself? You're not alone. One survey found that "97% of women have at least one negative thought about their bodies every day." (Kearney-Cooke, 2011). We've all suffered from having a negative body image at some point. That's the thing about low self-esteem. It can distort our sense of reality to the point where we don't see ourselves clearly at all. Having a negative body image is incredibly common, but that doesn't mean it's OK.

Someone I knew growing up would spend two hours every morning getting ready for school starting at age nine. The school had a uniform, so the clothes she was putting on were the same every day. That was two hours' worth of sleep or family time she wasn't getting done. I know she's not the only one. How many of us spend hours each week just on our outfits, makeup, jewelry, or hair? You are not to blame. Society can put a lot of pressure on looking good, and you probably just want to feel accepted (along with me and everyone else). But at what price are we willing to pay with our time, money, and mental health before enough is enough? I think a part of us is undoubtedly fed up with our value being tied to how we look. This certainly isn't the case for everyone, but it is prevalent enough to cause millions of people to doubt and judge themselves solely based on their appearance every day. The problem with this is that it gets in the way of your goals and how you see yourself.

Thankfully, that's a problem you and I can fix. Girls and guys alike feel the pressure to compare themselves to people (especially on social media). If you're going to post pictures, try to limit the amount of editing you do to the photos. Imagine all the younger kids who will see your pic and compare themselves to you, just like you might find yourself doing with others. Try not to post suggestive content, particularly if they're heavily edited. This is feeding into the problem of false perceptions. So many photos get posted online by people who are altering their appearance. This often comes across the wrong way and seems fake.

Focus on other areas in your life. I've realized that external beauty is not permanent and can be taken from you in an instant. After that car wreck on I-4, I realized how superficial many things are and how quickly they can be taken away. Since then, I've tried to prioritize what's important because very few things last in the looks department. What does live on is the impact you have on other people. If you're not feeling good about yourself, **volunteer** time to help others. Don't worry too much about what you look like because IT DOESN'T MATTER in the big scheme of things. How you feel on the inside is what makes you the most attractive.

Don't tolerate body shaming. I was talking with my friend one time when she brought up a story about my younger brother, Harrison. At first,

I was worried she would start listing off some of the infamous pranks he had pulled, but to my surprise, she agreed with me about what a good kid he was. She told me she talked with him about how the guys at her school rate girls on a scale of one to ten based on their looks. He got upset and told her how wrong that was for people to do. She told me she had never had any boy tell her that wasn't OK, and just hearing him say that made a big difference in how she saw herself and their behavior.

By just speaking out against body shaming, we can show people that it's wrong and help to stop it from occurring to more people. Be the person in someone else's life who cares enough to make a stand for what's right, even if it's not the popular decision. Compliment people on more than just their looks. This is a small way to let people know they have more value than just what's on the outside. Be with positive people. Who are you choosing to spend your time with daily? Are they obsessed with their looks? Are they confident in their beliefs and who they are? Wear clothes YOU like. Don't bother wearing things you don't feel comfortable in, and stick with what makes you feel confident about yourself. I've also found that wearing less makeup not only clears up my skin but makes me feel better about myself and less like I'm hiding behind a mask. Listening to body-positive music is also a great confidence booster. If you were to sit back and think about how subjective many song lyrics are, it's no wonder people place so much importance on how they look. Try listening to music that promotes a healthy image and isn't wrapped up in being so superficial.

Limit the time you spend getting ready. I have a rule (as extreme as it may sound) that the first outfit I put on for the day is the one I'm sticking with, pretty much no matter what. That way, I usually only spend around ten minutes getting ready each morning. I get that we want to look our best, but at what price are we willing to pay? Those who are only concerned about how you look will always just be focused on the outside and never about what truly matters. Look for people who care about more than just looks and I promise you will find them.

Focus on what you CAN control, such as your intelligence, self-worth, fitness level, and accomplishments. Stop saying negative things about your looks and instead focus on all the things you love about yourself. Finally, don't judge others on their appearance. By not putting weight on how others look, you're helping to put a stop to judging others based solely on appearance once and for all.

Anxiety & Depression

Anxiety and depression can become a massive barrier to becoming successful if you let them control your life. The key is being stronger than your fears and finding healthy ways to cope. Everyone gets down from time to time but knowing how to pull yourself back up again is what will help you achieve your goals. Spend energy focusing on what's important to you. Hang around positive people who have your best interests in mind. Make an effort to ignore negative thoughts and uplift positive ones.

Drugs, Smoking, Vaping, and Alcohol

No one denies that these substances are harmful, but it still doesn't stop people from using them. Maybe it's because they don't care or that the addictive power outweighs the consequences. Whatever the reasoning, stay away from substances that cause an unhealthy dependence. All it does is cause you to lose control over your own body. Why would you willingly give a substance power over you? It's best to stay away from addictive substances altogether because they WILL AFFECT YOUR GOALS no matter what. Avoid groups that normalize and give easy access to drugs, drinking, and alcohol. Have standards, and make sure to stick with friends who will respect your choices. If you already find yourself using certain substances, reach out to someone you trust to help right away.

Bullying

Bullying can be very inhibiting when trying to achieve your goals because it can make people feel undeserving and worthless. Anyone who holds some real or perceived power and tries to use it against you uses bullying behavior. I once had a girl who kicked me as hard as she could and told me I was ugly because she was angry I got the role she wanted in a play. I was going to ask the director for reassignment because I didn't want to get hurt again but decided against giving in so easily. Luckily, she didn't try anything after realizing I wouldn't be giving up and later apologized for her behavior. If you don't give bullying behavior any power over you, the person won't have anything they can use against you. No matter what, don't let them become obstacles in achieving your goals by allowing their negativity to win. Instead, stand up for yourself and others and fight for what's important to you.

I got my first real taste of bullying in preschool. Two kids decided to take over the school playground. The duo would claw at anyone who tried to climb up the monkey bars. Once, I made my way up, and they scratched the entire side of my face before shoving me down. This is symbolic of the struggle for many in life, and it doesn't matter who you are or how old you are. People WILL try to bully you and make you feel small. That's why it's so important to remember that *being teased has nothing to do with what you look like or who you are. It's entirely about the person bullying others*.

You can get a pretty good picture of how someone feels inside themselves by who they treat cruelly. For example, if someone is teasing you about being dumb, it's usually because they don't feel very smart themselves. Or maybe someone is calling you ugly because they don't feel pretty, even if you think they are. The truth about confident people is that they don't need to push other people down to feel good. They're usually those in the room who try to lift other people because they have enough love to share.

On the other hand, it's usually painfully obvious when people lack self-confidence because they try to push others down to try and make themselves feel better. Even if a person acts confident, it can sometimes just be arrogance in disguise. Arrogance is like a balloon swollen with air that could pop at any moment and is also easily deflated. It's usually to hide that the person has low self-esteem and may have even been bullied themselves. They might try to act sure of themselves when in reality, they're the least confident in the room. Maybe it's the jock loudly name-calling a player on the team or a girl mocking the way someone talks. Is that the kind of behavior someone would show if they felt good about themselves? Or is this the behavior of someone who is easily threatened by others?

Dealing With Rejection

Whether it's from a college or a crush, rejection is something we've all felt at some point in life. Learning to manage rejection in a healthy way can even help you use it as a source of motivation to achieve your goals. Don't let one person's 'no' deter you from success. If anything, each 'no' is just one step closer to the 'yes' you need. Take rejection in stride and put it in its place. The one thing you should never do is let it defeat you. There's a reason it didn't work out, and better things will eventually come your way soon if you're proactive in getting there. Many people take rejection as a signal to quit, but *it's those who persevere who succeed.*

Opposition comes in many forms, whether it's someone bullying you or a voice in your head saying you aren't good enough. Luckily, there's plenty of ways we can defeat people who doubt us by having unshakeable confidence, learning to care less about what others think, and sticking up for what we believe. Don't put up with people trying to push you around. Instead, fight back for your goals. Anything worth achieving in life won't always be easy, so stay true to yourself, and you'll be able to handle anything that comes your way.

CHAPTER 5:

FINDING HAPPINESS

*"Learn how to be happy with
what you have while you
pursue all that you want."*
—Jim Rohn

Finding internal happiness and sharing it with others is one of the most incredible things you can achieve. It means that no matter what you will or have already accomplished in life, you don't have to rely on external factors to be content. Whatever hardships you will face, they won't have the ability to control or define you. This chapter will work on forming a happy, healthy, and positive outlook on life. Happiness is something that can be learned and a mindset that can be refined. If we think of happiness like this, we realize it's something WE can control.

Unfortunately, the world we live in sometimes has a warped view of what makes people happy. Watching most Hollywood blockbusters and you might think happiness equals having tons of money, a sports car, and partying at all hours of the night in a mega-mansion. The reality is a lot of this is an attempt to cover up the fact that something is lacking in our society. Just think of the efforts in which people try and forget their pain, whether through drugs, alcohol, or parties. The sad part is this doesn't fix the real problem. It only makes it worse. So, when is it enough?

An excellent way to figure this out is by asking yourself what you want in life. Chapter One invited you to write down your dream life filled with precisely what you're striving to achieve. Trying to reach for more and accomplish big things is great, as long as that's what makes you happy. Think about the point of it all. What drives you to wake up in the morning and work toward your goals? Is it for money, fame, fear of failure, or something else? Working toward your goals and aspiring to be the best is great, but living a happy life helps give it meaning. If you love what you're doing and it makes you happy, it won't feel like work at all.

The Pitfalls of Success

Many people get stuck down this path where they're always striving for more no matter what they've achieved in their life. Many successful people struggle with this because it's what's driven them to be successful in the first place. This can be a great motivator, but some find that being able to finally shut off that mindset and enjoy what they've accomplished to be incredibly challenging. You have to determine when you've achieved exactly what you want for yourself, but an excellent way to figure this out is by asking yourself what you want in life. Once you've fulfilled what you've set out to do, knowing when and how to enjoy it is the next step. Otherwise, you may find yourself spinning instead of moving on to doing something more productive and living your best life.

I knew a man whose goal was to be worth $10 million. Once he achieved that, he immediately increased his goal to be worth $100 million. He told himself that he'd finally be happy once he got to his new goal, even though he already promised himself he'd be satisfied after the first $10 million. It got to the point where no matter how many zeros were at the end of his bank account, he was still miserable. He had spent all his time trying to grow his business when all he had really wanted was a family. As crazy as it sounds, he had never paused and looked around at what he wanted until it was almost too late. Don't make the same mistake he almost did by linking happiness to external things. With this mindset, nothing will ever be good enough. It's your life, and you have to find what brings you joy. Don't rely on other people or things to make you happy. Only you can do that.

"Finding" Happiness

Often you don't have to look far to find happiness. You may not have to *find* it at all. You can be happy right now with what you have. It doesn't mean you shouldn't stop striving for more; just that happiness is a feeling WE can control and create ourselves. It's easier to work toward more significant accomplishments when you feel at peace with what you've already worked hard to achieve. You know you've found internal happiness when you can look at what you already have and feel like it's enough. As basic as this sounds, very few people ever get to this point.

Happiness is one of the most challenging things because it's easy to get misdirected in an attempt to find it. I used to think that if I could get rid of my acne, lose a few pounds, or have a few more thousand followers on Instagram, *then* it all would "finally be good enough." What I realized is that with that attitude, nothing would ever be enough. I'd be spending my whole life chasing after 'things' and move on to more 'things' as soon as I got what I thought I wanted. I was looking for a sense of peace that little in this world truly provides. So, what does bring happiness? There are a lot of false perceptions of what people think will make them happy. Money. A nice car. A big house. It's true that these things certainly make it *easier,* but you have to be the one to choose to be happy at the end of the day. Looking like a Vogue model, being in a movie or dining at high-end restaurants **doesn't equal happiness**. What is this grand secret to being happy that money can't buy and only a few can find? I've used a **HACK to Happiness** involving four ways you can work on feeling better about yourself and what you've accomplished already to help you achieve even more incredible things.

So, here's your HACK:

Having a place where you feel safe and loved by the people around you.

Actively pursuing happiness.

Changing your outlook.

Knowing you are unconditionally loved by God.

The 'H'

Having a place where you feel safe and loved by the people around you

When working toward my goals, sometimes it meant I'd be away from my home for months on end. I used to dread thinking about all the fun things I was missing out on, like birthdays, fishing trips, and dances I'd never enjoy. While earning all the merit badges in 2019, I was gone for more than ten months. Even though I'd gone off on this wild adventure, what helped me succeed was knowing I would have a stable base where I could return home. We all need something or someplace where no matter what's going on in our lives, we're able to drop all our worries and feel safe without the pressures of the rest of the world. It could be a specific person, grandma's kitchen, or your hometown, but no matter where you are in life, you should know you can always have a place or a person that feels like home. Once you find something like this, don't let it slip through your fingers. Go off and do big things but remember the people who love you and places that helped shape you into the person you are today.

The 'A'
Actively pursuing happiness

Actively pursuing happiness takes work. Life has a way of feeling like it's constantly trying to drag you down, and we all have our uphill battles to face. When I was younger, I was very close with two of my family members. I would visit them at their farm, and we'd pick fruit and vegetables in their garden, make holiday cards, and feed the animals together. I have some great memories with them, but the majority aren't as lovely to remember. They both decided not to be a part of our family anymore and decided to stop all communication when I was a child. They actively chose not to show up to birthdays, Christmases, or significant events in our lives. The last time I saw them, I learned to ride a bike; now, I'm learning to drive a car and fly an airplane. It's crazy how fast time slips away. Many of my friends had family members who had passed away and would have given anything to be involved in their lives for a few more years. In my case, I never saw them again. One of them died of breast cancer just before this book was published.

We all have stories of pain and rejection, but they make us who we are. Either we learn from our experiences and grow stronger, or let our frustrations and grief consume us. It's hard to get back up and fight when we feel so overwhelmed, but it's something we must do. In my case, once I began looking on the bright side of a sad situation, I began to see all the blessings God had given me. I have two of the most amazing grandparents who have always been a huge part of my life, as well as a strong immediate family. Every day I know they choose to be with me, and that makes up for everything else.

It can feel like a weight being carried around on our shoulders when dealing with awful burdens such as abuse, violence, or death. Whatever your battle is in life, try to keep looking at the happiness that you do have (even if it feels like there isn't any). For example, if your loved one has died, know you'll be able to see them again. If you're a survivor of rape or assault, you've proven yourself more powerful than your abuser by not letting their horrible actions defeat you. Perhaps you can also help prevent it from happening to others and spread awareness about the issue. You are strong and WILL survive whatever comes your way in life. Even if it feels like the sadness, grief, and pain are too overwhelming to handle anymore, it will get better. Do not give up. Do not lose hope. Keep fighting, and I know you will succeed.

I'm not asking you to forget about the bad things that have happened. Some scars are just too deep and won't ever fully heal. To ask you to move on and "get over it" won't do you any good either. I'm simply asking you to look to the parts of your life that help make your world feel less dark and use it as a life jacket to get your head above the waves. You might still be in an ocean of sorrow or pain, but that doesn't mean you have to drown. Some days will be more painful than others, so you might need extra encouragement.

It might sound impossible now, but you can also use your hurt to channel your success. I knew two siblings whose older sister died from a rare medical condition. The death was so sudden that no one was able to say goodbye in time. Because of the loss, one sibling developed a severe drinking problem and quit college. The other threw herself into her schoolwork and ended up finishing her degree just like her big sister had wanted her to do. Both had to deal with the same loss and the same pain of losing a sibling, but one let grief destroy him, and the other used it as fuel to make her sister proud. In life, you can choose once you stumble to stay there on the ground, or you can pick yourself up and keep walking. It's up to you to decide.

The 'C'
Change your outlook

When life brings you challenging situations, try and look on the bright side, even if sometimes it doesn't feel like there is one. It can be challenging to try and be positive constantly. Over time though, it will become easier to find motivation, stay focused, and inspire others.

Having a positive outlook takes work. It takes training your mind. I naturally am a very optimistic person, which makes it easier to be positive, but it's also a learned mindset. Every day I choose to be positive, and sometimes that can be a struggle. When situations start to weigh me down and get negative, I rarely accomplish anything productive. Instead, by working to keep that positive mindset, it becomes so much easier to persevere and finish what needs to get done. Most of my friends have never seen the intensity I take with me when working on my goals. They would be surprised if I told them about sleeping on the ground for weeks on end, or hiking with a twisted ankle, or waking up with a ribcage so sore it's hard to breathe only to get up and train for hours on end. The reason is that I don't take that intensity with me when I'm in the suburbs grabbing pizza with my friends (at least I try not to ;). But the girl who is giggling her head off with her friends is the same one pulling ticks off her neck with a pair of tweezers while hiking the Appalachian Trail.

I try to have a positive attitude no matter where life takes me because the one thing I can count on is that my circumstances WILL change. For better or worse. What I can control is whether I have a positive or negative attitude and how I treat the people around me throughout it. Having a positive mindset is critical when it comes to achieving your goals. If you let yourself or others beat you down, it's so much harder to get where you're going. Work to keep a healthy mindset, and you will achieve so much more of your goals. Whatever you're up against, be it critics, an abusive relationship, or an emotional breakdown, do not let it beat you. There is a light at the end of the tunnel, and you will make it out of the darkness if you just keep driving.

The 'K'

One of the essential secrets to happiness is knowing that you are loved. As cheesy as it may sound, we all want to be loved and feel accepted at the end of the day. The best part about this is you don't have to go out and find love. It's already found you.

In the Bible, my favorite verses are 1 Corinthians 13:4-8 because it describes what love looks like from God. "Love is patient. Love is kind. It does not envy. It does not boast. It is not proud. It does not dishonor others. It is not self-seeking. It is not easily angered. It keeps no record of wrongs. Love does not delight in evil but rejoices with the truth. It always protects, always trusts, always hopes, always perseveres. Love never fails."

Imagine if we all were able to love other people this way. Many problems would become nonexistent if we lived in a world where everyone could love others as God does. Have you ever come across someone who compliments you and then adds something snide at the end? It's almost like they were trying to be nice but couldn't quite get there. Whenever I hear people do this, I find it usually means they don't feel loved enough in their own lives to feel like they can give any of it away to others. If you struggle with this, you're not alone.

I felt the same way until it dawned on me that God loves me unconditionally, no matter what I've done or will do. His love is patient, kind, humble, pure, honorable, selfless, slow to anger, protective, trusting, hopeful, perseveres, and NEVER fails. After realizing this, it was easier to be happy and give freely to others without feeling like I didn't have enough love to share. I finally felt content where I could help others feel the same.

Feeling loved by God without conditions and seeing it every day gives us true happiness inside that no one can take away. So how do you let God into your life? Spoiler alert: He's already in it. He already knows what you ate for breakfast, when your heart got broken in a bad relationship, and even your favorite movie quotes. He knows because He cares about you. We don't get to see that kind of love from people often because of how rare and pure it is. In a world where many relationships are based on a "what can you do for me" kind of mindset, knowing there's another way to give love is so refreshing to see. Unfortunately, many people get caught in situations where either one or both people are just trying to take advantage of the other. I ask you to think about what you can give, instead of just what you can get out of others. Strive to find people with a similar mindset.

Learning to not only feel unconditional love but share it with others is something I think we should all work towards because it's the way God loves us. Knowing you are loved like this is a huge accomplishment within itself because it takes realizing how special you are to God. The good news is that it becomes easy to love others when you feel loved yourself. Be willing to accept God's love, and you'll find yourself happier and more fulfilled. I used to think this kind of love didn't exist but look around at all the people in your life who consistently show up and are there for you no matter what. Those are the kind of people who love you the way you deserve to be treated. Your family, friends, teachers, coaches, and pastors should be some of the people you can count on to help you when you need them. Sometimes, a few of these people don't show you love in the right way or let you down, but that doesn't mean you aren't deserving. They're just not at a point in *their* lives where they can show love to other people in the right way. It's not a reflection of you.

Now that we've gone over some HACKs to happiness, it's important to develop some easy methods to apply to your life right now. There are hundreds of ways you can work on being a happier person. It's relatively easy to do once you form the proper habits.

Make sure your goals are things you want to accomplish. If you're doing something just to please other people, you're doing it for the wrong reasons. Find important things that you want to achieve, and you'll find yourself much happier when you do. Take time to reflect on your accomplishments before moving on is a crucial way to feeling fulfilled. If you're just hopping from one goal to the next, it can all begin to lose its meaning. Congratulate yourself and others after achieving your goals and you'll not only stay motivated but find yourself happier with your accomplishments.

Don't compare yourself to others.
Doing BIG is about accomplishing what YOU set out to do in life. It's different for different people. My definition of success could look like living in a house on the beach with the people I love, whereas yours could mean being the CEO of a Fortune 500 Company and worth millions of dollars. By comparing yourself to other people, you're setting up unfair and unrealistic expectations for yourself. Of

course, there will be people in this world with more money, a bigger house, or more followers on social media, but that doesn't make them any more or less successful than you are. All it means is that they've prioritized other things and that their definition of success is different than yours. By recognizing this, hopefully, you'll be able to stop unrealistically comparing yourself to others and focus on adopting a healthier mindset instead.

Spend time doing things you want.

Taking the things that make you happy and then incorporating them into your goals is a great way to stay motivated and feel fulfilled. Find something you love doing, and the rest will be a whole lot easier to accomplish. It's impossible to avoid doing things you don't want to do, but finding a healthy balance will help you stay happy. If you dread trying to accomplish your goals, you need to reassess them. Remember that your goals should reflect things you enjoy doing and look forward to working on.

Work hard, play hard.

My family has a strategy that we've used for generations. It's the idea that if you work hard and accomplish BIG things, you need to have BIG rewards too. If anything drove me to be successful and feel content, it's this mentality. Since I tend to be a workaholic, it can be hard for me to take breaks when working on a project. By giving myself some time off (even if just for a few minutes), I can get more work done and stay motivated. In my family, we call them 'carrots.' A lot of people hold out those carrots, or prizes, that they promise themselves after completing a task and then never end up rewarding themselves. If life becomes all work and no play, there's no motivation and no point to keep working. It's important to enjoy what you've accomplished because life is short and living it to the fullest is a form of success in itself. This mindset helps to create a balance where you can pause and reflect on your goals as well. If you work hard, you should push yourself to do the best you can. If you're playing hard, go on amazing adventures and reward yourself with fun experiences you'll never forget. Above all, focus on finding internal happiness where you are right now in your journey. Know that whatever comes your way, nothing will take away the great memories and experiences you were able to have in your life. This shouldn't stop you from striving for more, but it should make you focus your energy on what you want to achieve and give you the motivation to get there.

In this chapter, we covered how you can find happiness in your own life regardless of your current circumstances. The choice is yours to make, and once you do, things will get easier just by changing your mindset. From that point forward, you can focus on living life to the fullest despite the setbacks, sadness, and tragedy you've faced. It doesn't mean you have to move on or try to forget what's happened, just that you keep working to persevere even when you're ready to quit. Being happy WON'T occur just because you get more stuff, make more money, or move into a bigger house.

The truth is people can be miserable anywhere, just like they can be satisfied anywhere. The decision is YOURS to make. How will you choose to go about living your life? By trying to have a more positive attitude about things (whether I wanted to do them or not), I found I could get things done faster and had a better time doing them.

As cringeworthy as it may sound, striving to stay optimistic about things makes everything a lot easier. Finding true happiness and peace is what we're all looking for at the end of the day. Some of us go about looking for it at parties, by spending money, or at the bottom of a bottle, but at least in my life, I've found very few things 'give' you happiness. What does provide you with joy is the mindset of realizing and accepting that you are loved. The best part about this is that you don't have to go out trying to *find* it. It's already found you. God loves you without conditions, regardless of what you have or what you do in your life. He loves you despite your flaws. You are perfectly created in His image and are precisely the way you're supposed to be. You don't need to go searching for happiness and love because it's already inside you.

And remember your HACK to Happiness:

Having a place where you feel safe and loved by the people around you

Actively pursuing happiness

Changing your outlook

Knowing that you are loved

DO BIG!

CHAPTER 6:

HEALTHY RELATIONSHIPS

*"I used to think the worst
thing in life was to end up all
alone. It's not. The worst thing
in life is to end up with people
that make you feel all alone."*
—Robin Williams

A whole chapter dedicated to relationships might seem a little strange for a goal-setting book, but the people we let into our lives can significantly impact who we are, what we do, and who we will become. That's why it's so important to know who has our best interests in mind so we know who we should and should not trust. When working on accomplishing BIG things, surrounding yourself with people who will have your back, no matter what can make a world of difference. This chapter is broken into two sections. The first part is on friendship and family, and the second is on romantic relationships. Both shape us and our lives, so it's essential we carefully choose who we let get close to us because they will end up affecting our goals and decisions.

Friendship & Family

The truth is I would not have been able to achieve as much as I have in such a short time had it not been for the people in my life who I know I can count on (namely my family). When I use the term family, I'm not just talking about blood relatives. Just because you're related to someone doesn't mean they'll treat you the way they should. Family is someone you can count on to be present in your life and have your back. Family is the people who care about and love you for who you are. They help you when you need it and vice versa. Someone who's a part of your "family" could be a close friend, sibling, coach, mentor, parent, or grandparent. It's someone you can trust enough to have a significant impact and say in your life. That's why the people you choose to be in your life have such weight in reaching your goals. Determining who you can and can't trust will save you so much heartache and pain that it's one of the most critical skills you'll ever need.

I once thought that people would get nicer as I got older, and as much as I wish that were the case, people will still be cruel. I've learned that I can only count on a handful of people to be loyal, and I'm very blessed to have that many. For you, I hope that number is much higher, but the reality is you only need a few good people to make a difference.

When I talk about people you can trust, I don't just mean someone who won't tell all your secrets. I mean somebody who's like a dive buddy. In SCUBA diving, your "buddy" looks out for you and vice versa. If you run out of air, they're supposed to let you use some of theirs until you both make it back to the surface. Picking a dive buddy is a big deal because you are entrusting them with your life. If you think of trust that way, we would probably only have a couple of people we would feel comfortable having in that position. Think of all your "friends" and who would fulfill that responsibility, and then you know you've found someone who'll have your back.

Sadly, the more successful you become, the more others may see you as a threat. That's why keeping your true friends and family close is so important. A great way to find out if someone has your back is by seeing how they treat others. To tell whether someone is trustworthy, go with your gut. The way that people treat others is also a great way to figure this out. If they're mean to you or others, that's not a good sign. A part of working toward success is that you will come across many people who don't have your best interests in mind. You might not even realize the effects they've had on you until it's too late. That is why it's so important to identify negative influences so you can distance yourself from them before they intentionally or unintentionally hurt you.

What are some signs of a bad influence? One of the biggest red flags is if they make you feel bad about yourself. You don't need that kind of negativity in your life because it can start to snowball and affect you in ways you might not even see. Some classic signs of a bad influence are if they're drinking and driving, using illegal substances, getting into fights, smoking or vaping, or breaking the law. These should be huge warning signs that this person doesn't even have their own best interests in mind and certainly won't have yours either.

I had someone in my life who would try and pressure me into doing things I wasn't comfortable with doing. We've all had that one "friend" who tries to do this, but what I realized is that *real friends would never intentionally pressure you into things you aren't OK doing.* You must distance yourself from bad influences like this before they drag you down too.

You may be able to help them even more from a distance. Think of it as a sinking ship. By jumping onto the ship, you aren't doing anyone any good. On the other hand, if you were to throw the people onboard a life ring from onshore, you could pull them to safety without the risk of drowning yourself. Another sign of a negative influence is someone who tries to manipulate you. Many people have had to deal with this, which is why it's so important to recognize what it looks like so you can help prevent it.

I had a close friend who tried to help a person, and in trying to do the right thing, she found herself in a bad situation. The person began texting her regularly and started taking up more and more of her time and energy as she attempted to help him with all his problems. She would get texts and calls at all hours of the night and show up exhausted whenever we'd get together. His problems were weighing heavily on her, but she was "too afraid to speak up" because she didn't want to hurt him or have him hurt himself. Soon though, she realized she was being manipulated when he tried to persuade her that getting into a relationship was the only way he wouldn't kill himself. Finally, she stuck up for herself and broke off all communication after ensuring he got the help he needed. It was important to her to include this story in the book because many people are being manipulated in similar ways and don't even know it. It can be frightening to think that someone is using your emotions to try and control you, but it happens ALL THE TIME.

How do you stop people from using you to get what they want? The first step is to recognize what's going on. It can be tricky to figure out whether people's intentions are genuine or not, but there are a few ways to tell. One way is if the relationship is entirely one-sided. This can apply to friends, family, or partners. If they seem to only talk about themselves, or ask about your day just so they can tell you how awful theirs was, these should be red flags.

Remember, if your needs aren't being met, they're just taking without giving anything in return. These relationships are hard to maintain for a reason. THEY'RE UNHEALTHY! It causes stress, anxiety and can create more problems than it does solutions. People will try to control you for all sorts of reasons, whether to make themselves feel better, gain power, or get something out of you. It's important to recognize this and to keep the people who have your best interests in mind close to you. To maintain boundaries, you must be persistent. Don't give in if someone is doing something you aren't comfortable doing. It's your life, and you need to take control of it, or others will take control of it for you. If someone's using bullying behavior in any way, this is not someone you want to have in your life. This will only lead to an unhealthy downward spiral that causes you to lose sight of what matters.

Now that we know the things NOT to look for in forming friendships with other people, let's look at the qualities of a true friend. Many people want to be your friend when you're ahead in life, but very few stick around when things get tough. My mom always tells me that the best way to find out who your real friends are is by imagining you have to load a moving truck. The people you know you could count on to show up to help are the ones who aren't fair-weathered friends. They'll be there for you when you need it and not just when everything's fine and dandy. These are the people you want to invest time and energy in building a relationship with because they're in your life for the right reasons. They'll help you up when you need it and won't push you down if they get the chance.

The same should be something we strive to become. We need to be the kind of friend we want to have. It can be hard to give to people because there are so many times it can come back to bite you. That doesn't mean you should stop being nice to people. If anything, it's a reminder of how much people need to see the defining characteristics of a real friend. Be the person others look up to because of the kindness you show to others, and you will find that the people in your life will follow suit.

Now that you know what to look for, learning how to become their friend is the next step. For some, this might sound easy. For others, it can be a stressful and daunting task. Either way, making friends and forming connections with others is a critical life skill that will come in handy when working on your goals.

How to make friends is a skill that's rarely taught. Instead, most children are just left to fend for themselves when it comes to forming relationships with other people. It took me a while to get to the point in my life where being a good friend to others was even possible. I realized that most of us aren't born with the ability to go out and make and keep friends instantly, and it can take a lot of work to learn how to be a good friend. Some people are naturally better at doing this, but it can be quite a challenge for others.

Making friends isn't that hard if you break it down. Work up the nerve to walk over and introduce yourself. Start with your name and ask for theirs. Then, try and find common ground. You can do this based on what they're wearing, what they're doing, or by something you know about them.

Ask the person open-ended questions. If you're struggling to come up with some, come up with a list and memorize it. Holding conversations with people you don't know is a critical skill worth the effort to develop. From there, if you want to pursue a friendship, you can ask them for their contact information or make plans to meet up.

If you're nervous about getting rejected or even teased, don't be. That's just a part of life, and you can't care too much about being shot down because there will always be people in life who will do that. Take it in stride and move on if that's the case. An important thing to note is that you don't have to be friends with everyone. If someone has no interest in becoming friends with the awesome person you are, don't take it personally and try to respect their wishes. They might not be at a point in their life where that's possible for them, or you both might not have much in common. That doesn't mean you can't be friendly. Even if someone has made it clear they don't want to develop a friendship, you should still treat them with common courtesy and move on to other people. Don't let someone's negative attitude deter you from making friends with others.

When I met one of my best friends for the first time, they were not what I expected. We knew each other for years before becoming friends. This is partly because I had written them off as being a certain way instead of taking the time to get to know them. That was my mistake. Don't automatically presume something about someone based on rumors or cliques. Instead, try to get to know the person first, and you might be pleasantly surprised.

There are also four "types" of friends. The first is an acquaintance. They're someone you might have a few interactions with but don't know much about their lives. The next type is a casual friend. In this stage, you both plan on meeting up and invest in getting to know each other better. A close friend takes it a step further by adding an emotional investment to the relationship. Both you and your friend know about each other's life goals, values, dreams, and ambitions, and there are very few, if any, secrets between you two. Having an intimate friend means you've both opened up to each other and been vulnerable to share and accept each other's flaws. It's rare to get this close with someone, but once you do, you know you'll have a friend for life.

Sometimes, the best types of friendships can come from shared experiences. My brother met this boy in New York, and the three of us became almost inseparable the whole camp. We'd all head down the trails to class together, singing and making jokes. For some reason, the boy had packed a wide variety of pots that he promptly gave out to put on our heads for our club. I politely declined (mine had bacon grease stuck to the bottom), but my brother immediately adopted his makeshift ball cap. So, if you were to watch us on our way to class, you would see two eleven-year-olds with pots on their heads singing "God Bless the USA" at the top of their lungs and a thirteen-year-old girl with a massive stack of worksheets singing along. We were an odd sight. At the end of camp, we all hugged goodbye but not before the boy offered a few words and asked for our address, saying, "I don't know if my mom will let me, but I'll try to mail the pot to your house." Apparently, that's a strange thing to say around a roomful of adults.

So how can you become an even more amazing friend? It involves **standing up for the other person** even if it makes you less popular. I was with one of my friends when a few girls came up and started teasing him. Even though the girls were in my class, I wasn't going to sit by and let them pick on my other friend. If you find yourself in this situation, do what you know is right, and things will be so much easier in the long run. You can't always be loyal to everyone all the time. In that situation, I found my loyalty between the girls tested when it meant standing up for my friend instead. Even though it meant committing 'social suicide,' it's just a part of the whole friendship deal.

Being a friend also means showing interest in their daily lives. **Ask your friend about their day** and **listen to what they have to say**. Being a good listener is a great way to be a friend to somebody. Try to avoid butting in with your own opinions and focus on **remembering what they're saying**.

Find ways you can **let the people in your life know they matter to you**. After getting into that serious car wreck when I was younger, I've always tried to let other people know they are important. I'll write cards to all my friends and family telling them how much they mean to me for holidays. The reason is that I never want to go through life regretting that I wasn't upfront with people about how I felt. Even if it means handwriting dozens of cards every year, it's something I always try and take the time to do.

Be the positive voice in your friend's life. Sometimes it's hard to see what other people are going through, especially if they don't want to talk about it. The best way you can show your support is by being the one who encourages. There will be lots of people in life (as you already know) who will try and push you down. Don't be that person for someone else. Be one of the very few who is a bright light in an often dimly lit world and who will encourage people when they need to hear it. Sometimes just having a few key people believing in us is enough to motivate people to do great things.

Don't stop yourself from saying how you feel. I used to try and hold my tongue when telling people how I felt because I didn't want to come across as weird or overly emotional. But the truth is that I'm definitely weird no matter how you slice it, and I'd much rather go through life being honest and upfront with people than trying to keep up an image that doesn't matter in the big scheme of things. For example, if you're grateful for someone's friendship, but a part of you wants to play it cool, just tell them how you feel! Let them know you value them as a friend and feel like the special person they are.

I remember when one of my friends first started a YouTube channel. I was so proud of her! I walked up to her, gave her an enormous hug, and told her what a brilliant idea I thought it was. Almost immediately, a bunch of other teens came over and began telling her how "dumb it was going to be" and that there was no way they were ever going to watch it. I was so angry! Here was someone trying to make a difference, and they were trying to make her feel bad to get a few laughs. Everyone's entitled to their opinions, including you. So, the next time you hear people trying to make someone else feel small, don't tolerate it. It's easy to be the person who's always negative and pushing people down.

The challenge is being the one who will support people even if it means being less popular.

Don't try to change your friend. We all have those things we wish we could change about somebody. But, unless someone is doing something illegal or bad for their health, *love your friends enough to accept them because of their flaws and not despite them*. **Be nice to their friends and family** as well. For some reason, I see this a lot where people think it's OK to treat me with respect but be nasty to my younger siblings. I do not tolerate that kind of behavior at all. Family comes first. By recognizing this about people, it will be easier to get along with your friends, no matter how annoying their siblings might be at times.

To keep friendships and solve conflicts, you must **be willing to work through misunderstandings**. You may be in sticky situations with your friends at times, but you have to be willing to work through it. Perhaps if there's something you need to get off your chest or talk about, you and your friend can do laps around the football field until you come up with a solution. Often the drama of a situation and how you handle it together make a friendship stronger. The key to any long-lasting friendship is to have open communication with each other. Both people have to be willing to compromise and find solutions. Especially with friends, you both know how to push each other's buttons, so it's so important never to use this knowledge to hurt them intentionally.

Romantic Relationships

Whether it's a crush on someone in class or a dramatic breakup, relationships can sometimes be *distracting*. Ok, that's an understatement. They can be *very distracting*. And all-consuming. Having a relationship with someone on top of trying to achieve your goals can undoubtedly be a challenge, so it's essential to find a healthy balance. It's also important to decide what's best for you. If you already have a supportive relationship going and can balance everything out without shortchanging yourself and your goals, that's awesome. Teach me your ways. Unfortunately, for many of us, there's rarely enough time to be great at all your roles. Being a good girl/boyfriend, successful student, an active member of the family, employee, a doer of chores and runner of errands, AND still having time to achieve all your other goals is a significant accomplishment. Not to mention finding someone who treats you with the respect you deserve.

Recently, I had the option of dating someone, but to be in a good relationship, I would have had to sacrifice a lot of my other goals. I decided against it because I didn't have the time to make it work. I was worried I would lose his friendship, but I knew it was the right decision in my heart. In the end, he said he'd never want to be responsible for holding me back from my goals, and now our friendship is even stronger. I will always be grateful to him for recognizing this and proving himself a true friend.

If someone has your best interests in mind, they will never want to become an obstacle for you. There are people out there who will respect your accomplishments without bringing you down, so focus on maintaining those relationships. Don't worry. People like this do still exist in the world. If you're going to have a relationship with anyone, have it with someone who respects your ambitions enough to let you pursue them. You, in turn, need to respect them enough to realize your limitations. Don't bother trying to be in a serious relationship if you're not at a point in your life where that's possible for you. I'm not saying you shouldn't date or have relationships with people, just that it's hard to have a meaningful relationship with someone and become successful in achieving all your goals at the same time if you're both not willing to compromise a little.

A lot of pop culture today shows a very unrealistic view of people's relationships. Often in movies, the girl or boy is never stressed, has flawless skin, perfect grades, is in great shape, and somehow has enough time to always hang out at the drop of a hat. In real life, you can only put so much time into pursuing a relationship before it affects other areas of your life. By just waiting until you've accomplished your goals before getting into a serious relationship, you can save yourself so much wasted time, energy, bitterness, and hurt.

My friend was heavily involved with her boyfriend, and they talked every day. They'd hang out after school and planned their whole lives out together. Sounds pretty romantic, right? It turns out her boyfriend had been cheating on her the entire time and was only making all these promises to get what he wanted. Because she had put so much stock in someone else, she was devasted when he failed to come through. How many times have we all heard this story before? Imagine if she had taken that time and energy and put it into achieving some of her goals instead. She would not only have a whole lot of accomplishments to show for it, but she also would have saved herself some heartbreak.

That won't be your narrative if you focus on bettering yourself first. The best part is, the more successful you become in your ambitions, the more people will admire and respect you for what you've accomplished. One of the best pieces of advice I've ever received is to "become the person you want to date." By becoming successful yourself, you won't be dependent on anyone else. Believe me when I say that people will want to date you when you have your life together and know what you want.

What then are some ways to avoid getting distracted by relationships when working on your goals? First, **reassess if you're at a point in your life where getting into a relationship is a good idea**. Your time is precious, so make sure you use it well. That doesn't mean you shouldn't have fun, just that you prioritize where most of your energy goes. If you're feeling emotionally drained from a relationship that won't likely go anywhere, then pull the plug! You don't need that in your life, and it'd be a better use of your time to focus on self-improvement instead.

Don't Tie Your Self-Worth to Other People's Opinions.

People often look to date someone in an attempt to solve their problems, but you shouldn't be looking to get involved with someone if you don't have your life in order first. Have enough self-respect to take the time to prioritize your needs. Focus on getting good grades, staying in shape, reading Scripture, volunteering, and feeling good about yourself. Only when you can successfully balance your goals should you add to the list by getting in a serious relationship with someone.

I know a girl who told me the real reason she went out on so many dates is that she wanted to feel good about herself. Eventually, she found she was letting random guys determine her self-esteem. Don't tie your worth to whether someone thinks you're attractive, or funny, or cute. If that's the case, focus on building up your self-confidence first instead of trying to find that from other people.

Make Time for Your Needs.

Dating takes work. Take time to consider the importance of this relationship versus the importance of your goals. How could this relationship sidetrack your goals? The biggest reason I've heard from my friends on why they go on dates so young is that "my soulmate could be sitting right in front of me in class, and I'll never know for sure unless I try." Statistically, most high school relationships don't go anywhere. Only 2% get married, and only about half of that stay married (Gaille, 2017). If a relationship doesn't work out, then THERE'S A REASON. Trust that God has a plan for you and will bring the right person into your life at the right time. Don't stress about relationships or dating. Go and live your life, and God will bring the right person into it when you're both ready.

Forming and maintaining healthy relationships is a critical part of achieving your goals. Not only for having a balanced lifestyle but also for making connections and working with others. No matter where life takes you, being able to make friends, understanding people's motives, and finding positive people will come in handy time and time again.

Each relationship we have in life can shape and teach us something new. From making friends to romantic partners, who we let into our life is an essential factor in our goals. Finding good people to share your life with may prove to be one of the most challenging things you'll come across. Some get lucky with a loving, supportive family and great friends, while others have yet to meet these people. Regardless, our family and friends significantly impact our goals, aspirations, and even personalities. They help shape us into the people we are and will become, which is why it's so important we choose wisely who we want in our lives. From there, being able to build a bond with the people in life that matter will prove to be an invaluable skill you'll use for the rest of your life.

CHAPTER 7:
PROTECTING YOURSELF AND YOUR GOALS

*"Self-defense is not just a
set of techniques; it's a state
of mind, and it begins with
the belief that you are worth
defending."*
—Rorion Gracie

We've all been hurt by somebody. I wish I could take away all the pain people have caused you, but the best we can do now is work through it together. Whether your story was marked with friends betraying you, assault, or even human trafficking, know that none of this is your fault. No matter your circumstances, I can promise that you are loved and worth defending. We'll cover everything from basic self-defense to what abuse looks like, so you'll be able to identify and protect yourself and your goals from the negative influences in your life once and for all.

Self Defense Techniques

Over years of training in martial arts, I learned specific techniques to help protect myself and others. Early on, I learned most self-defense didn't involve winning a fight in a one-on-one, movie-style confrontation. That's *not* really how the real world works. Crippling kicks, armbars, and perfectly landed punches won't do you any good if someone has slipped a sedative in your drink. I do suggest you study ways to defend yourself. Learning a form of martial arts is great discipline, and a combination of different styles allows you to have a variety of options if you're in danger. If that doesn't interest you though, there are many common-sense safety tips you can apply to your life right now to help keep yourself, your loved ones, and your goals safe.

Trust your instincts. The best self-defense tactic is to be aware of your surroundings. **Avoid going places alone** and **tell people where you plan to go**. It doesn't matter if you're a senior in high school or a senior citizen. Using common sense when it comes to keeping yourself safe is usually enough to avoid most circumstances. If you are in a situation where you need to protect yourself, **aim for vulnerable areas** such as the ears, eyes, nose, throat, groin, and kneecaps. Use an open palm to strike instead of a fist, so you don't break your fingers.

Fight back with anything you have and **draw attention** by yelling, screaming, and thrashing. If you're younger or lighter and someone is trying to take you somewhere against your will, shout something along the lines of "Help! I don't know this person!" Or even, "Fire!" That phrase draws people toward you because they want to see the trouble! Bite, tear, rip, and claw your way free. If you're small enough to be picked up and dragged, **use dead weight** to your advantage. This is when your body goes completely limp, and it becomes harder to move you.

If you're a child, know there is no reason an adult should be coming to ask you for help. If someone needs help with directions or finding their dog, just politely—and from a distance—tell them that you don't know and move away from there. It is OK to be rude to an adult you don't know who is approaching you.

Most confrontations don't usually go this way. Like predators in the wild, most people won't want to exert the energy or risk getting into a fight. So, things like drink spiking are a more common threat, especially for women. I know several teenage girls in my circle of friends who have already had this happen to them. It's impossible to avoid many of these situations, but we can make it as hard as possible for people to do this to you. Always go places with a friend, pour your own drink if possible, or take your beverages with you. Check the lid on any bottle of water to make sure the seal has not been broken. Never accept drinks from strangers and report it immediately if you saw someone spike a drink. Go out with people you know will look out for you and do the same for them. You can also use a resealable cup like a water bottle when going places and avoid using anything that could inhibit your public senses.

Bring your phone with you and use apps that allow your location to be monitored by friends and family. Research how your type of phone provides ways to call emergency services, such as by clicking the wake button five times. You can pretend to be on your phone when walking to your car or in other situations where you feel uncomfortable.

Keep your device in an easily reachable place, such as in your pocket, bag, or in your hand.

If you're meeting up with someone for the first time, you can do a quick search online beforehand to make sure everything checks out, which nowadays is practically standard operating procedure. The best way I've found to avoid many dangerous circumstances is by hanging out with people who have your best interests in mind. That way, they'll look out for you and vice versa. It's harder for predators to get to someone in a group. If you're driving, avoid parking in dimly lit areas. Never drink and drive, and always keep your car doors locked. If you're followed, pull into a police station, hospital, or similar high-traffic area. Hide electronics, money, purses from plain view and carry a (legal) form of self-defense in your vehicle.

Finally, avoid talking to strangers. And if you're a man who is approaching a woman, keep that in mind. For women, having a stranger come up to them can cause a lot of stress. If you're a guy, you can make a difference by simply respecting this about women and help us feel more comfortable. For the girls and women reading this, don't tolerate something if it makes you feel uncomfortable. If someone has said or done something inappropriate, remove yourself from the situation as soon as possible. Don't worry about being polite if you don't feel safe. It's better to know you're out of harm's way.

Protecting Yourself Mentally

There are many physical threats, but by far, some of the most harmful dangers are the ones we can't always see. To achieve your goals, you need to be strong both mentally and physically. This means knowing what you should let affect you and what shouldn't. There are plenty of people who will try and persuade you that you aren't enough in whatever you're working to accomplish. It's so important to tune these voices out and focus on getting where you need to go. The key to being able to protect yourself mentally is by being able to guard your heart.

In the Bible, Solomon (the king of Israel) warns his son, saying, "Above all else, guard your heart, for everything you do flows from it. Keep your mouth free of perversity; keep corrupt talk far from your lips. Let your eyes look straight ahead; fix your gaze directly before you. Give careful thought to the paths for your feet, and be steadfast in all your ways. Do not turn to the right or the left; keep your foot from evil." (Proverbs 4:23-27).

Solomon is telling his son this to defend himself from people looking to hurt him. He doesn't want his son to leave his heart unprotected because all his talents and gifts flow through it. Guarding your heart doesn't mean you have to be cold and closed off to the rest of the world or not trust people. Instead, it's a way to slowly let people and things get close to you after they've proven themselves to be deserving of your trust. God doesn't want us to become wounded from the negativity of others, so He teaches us how to protect ourselves. You can still be open and accepting of others, but careful about who you let get close enough to hurt you. Allowing others' negativity to roll off your shoulders is one of the most remarkable skills you can possess. It means you'll be able to achieve what you want without outside voices belittling or pushing you down.

Facing Your Fears

Fear is a powerful emotion. It can drive people to succeed and cause others to do terrible things. If we can learn to harness our anxiety and defeat it, we take away its ability to limit our decisions. Fear can be of a person, a place, an animal, a thing, or even an emotion like love. Whatever your fear is, it's probably more complex than the monster under your bed at night when you were a child. Maybe you're afraid of being attacked again, losing a loved one, or dying. The scariest fears are the valid ones where you can't just plug in a nightlight to make it go away, but that doesn't mean you should let it reign over your life either. This section is about being able to face your fears to focus on succeeding in your goals. We'll go over managing anxiety, everyday worries, unhealthy distractions, and ways to cope with fear.

I used to be terrified of jellyfish, which makes things challenging when some of my favorite hobbies are scuba diving, sailing, and underwater photography. I wouldn't go in the ocean past my waist for years despite living on a peninsula, and I obsessively learned everything I could about the species. While on a dive trip to The Florida Keys, I was underwater exploring an old shipwreck. Suddenly, I looked up and saw hundreds of jellies surrounding me. I almost had a mini heart attack; I was so scared! But the one thing you should never do while breathing from a limited amount of condensed air while at the bottom of the ocean is panic, so I worked on staying as calm as I could. My dive buddy and I slowly began to ascend, trying not to get entangled in their tentacles.

As I slowly ascended, I saw the jellyfish in a new light. They were so peaceful as they floated through the current that they *calmed me down*. After reaching the dive boat, I had multiple stings across my body, but I was distracted by the peaceful plume of jellies drifting along the surface. The boat captain said he'd never seen so many jellies at once. Talk about a way to overcome your fear instantly. I realized that living my life in fear of something was no way to live at all. I had let my fears control me instead of the other way around.

We're all afraid of something, whether it's of getting rejected again, heights, or, yes, jellyfish. If we learn to control that fear, we can make sure it doesn't get in the way of achieving our goals and even use it to motivate us. For many of us, what scares us are the things we can't touch. Fear of dying or losing a loved one. Fear of not succeeding. Fear of being all alone. It's these concerns that can sit in the back of our minds and cause us to make the wrong decisions to avoid facing our fears. Even though those fears may be more realistic than a random jellyfish attack, it doesn't give them the right to control your life. We can beat them by learning to manage our anxiety and focus on making the right decisions when it counts.

Many people are terrified to get back into a relationship when they've been hurt in the past. It takes time to heal after someone or something has hurt us, and we have to live with the fact that we may never fully recover. Whatever your fears are, you don't have to try and bury them so they don't affect you. Instead, let them shape your choices in a healthy way instead of a harmful one.

I had someone in my life who would yell at me when I was a little girl. When I was older, whenever I heard someone yelling, I quickly relapsed into feeling like that small and defenseless girl again who couldn't stand up or fight back. The truth is I could have, but I was too afraid to do anything about it. Over the years, I've had to find ways to manage anxiety if I was going to achieve my goals. I couldn't be too afraid of heights if I was going to fly planes, jellyfish while diving, being yelled at or kicked while earning my black belt, or anything else that threatened to become too controlling. The solution I've found is that **you must work with and through fears, not against them.** We're afraid of these things for a reason, and many times that's a good thing. If it's a healthy fear, you shouldn't stop trying to be afraid of it. Instead, work within your limitations.

Managing Stress and Anxiety

Some of the best memories I have are from Scout camp. One time during lunch, a bunch of us went down to the creek to go fishing. One of the kids had stuffed hot dogs from the kitchen into his pockets to use as bait, and we pulled out some fishing line and hooks. We all went into the forest to get some sticks and sat down on the dock. It felt like living in *The Adventures of Tom Sawyer*. We were able to hide in the mountains of Georgia and fish all day, far from the pull of the world. It was here that there became such camaraderie between kids who hadn't known each other just a few days earlier. We just sat side by side with our toes in the cool stream and our eyes glued to the ripples in the water. Back in the modern world, where people are worried about everything from grades to global pandemics, you realize how special these moments are.

Life can and will be filled with lots of stress. One of the secrets to success is knowing how to manage stress to accomplish your goals. Know that stress and anxiety affect almost everyone at some point. It's OK if you're feeling the weight of some of your tasks. That can be a good thing because it means you're taking things seriously. If it feels like too much, it's time to take control of your worries and get back on course.

If you're feeling anxious about something, **spend time with people who calm you down**. Find friends with who you can have fun and make plans together.

Break tasks up. I would often write to-do lists, and they caused a lot of stress until I realized I was writing them wrong! I would group HUGE tasks into a few words like 'finish book' or 'get pilot's license' Any one of these tasks can take months or even years to complete. What I needed to do instead was split things up more. That way, I'd see how much I was accomplishing and help alleviate some pressure.

Make a checklist of essential things you need to get done each day. As you go through each item, you'll feel so much better when you look back and see how much you've been able to accomplish.

Don't be afraid to take breaks. Taking a break and stepping away is a great way to come back ready to work. Sometimes just going for a walk or getting something to eat will do wonders if you're dealing with something stressful.

Speaking of eating, make sure to **have healthy food**. It is so much easier to deal with anxiety on a full stomach rather than on an empty one. The food you do put in your body should be packed with nutrients to help you focus. Eating "junk food" has even been linked to increased stress, so stay away from it as much as possible. I know this is easier said than done, but it's worth a shot to see how it makes you feel.

Don't work where you sleep. This is a huge factor when it comes to getting a good night's rest. I'm on my computer a lot for school or writing, and I often would find myself lying in bed while working. I began having problems sleeping, and it never seemed to feel like I could take breaks. I'd often wake up in the middle of the night and work instead of getting a decent night's sleep. Having a separate space where you work and where you sleep is critical to curbing anxiety, and I guarantee you'll notice a difference right away.

Exercise regularly. Not only is this a great way to clear your thoughts, but it also boosts your energy levels and keeps you in shape. I also go to the gym to take a mental break and think about the tasks ahead.

Don't be afraid to vent from time to time. If something's stressing you, one of the best ways to rationalize your fears is by talking about it. Having someone you can bounce ideas off of can help ground you and get you back on track.

Eliminate triggers. If someone or something causes you to get nervous or lose focus in an unhealthy way, try distancing yourself for a while. I used to spend time with some girls who were awful to me. Instead of working on my goals, I got stuck in a loop thinking about why they hated me so much and what I could do to fix it. What I later realized is how much time I had wasted worrying about a problem I couldn't fix in the first place. If people are causing you unnecessary stress or anxiety, you don't need to have them in your life. Even if you see them every day at school, stop giving what they say or do any weight. Focus on distancing yourself from them, both physically and emotionally.

While these are great ways to manage fears, how do you get to the point of overcoming them? It's important to determine whether your fear is real. You can do some simple things like Googling the likelihood of the event occurring. For example, if you're afraid of getting attacked by a shark, you'll find that to be VERY unlikely to happen. Particularly on land! On the other hand, if you're worried about getting raped, this, unfortunately, is a much more rational fear, with about 25% of girls and 16% of boys being sexually assaulted before the age of eighteen. (Finkelhor, et al., 1990)

It's also important to determine if your fear is healthy. Being worried about something and taking reasonable safety measures to prevent it is normal. If you find yourself to the point where you let your fears negatively affect your life, it's time to stop letting your fears control you and your goals. If you've found your anxiety to be unrealistic and unhealthy, realize you are not alone. Millions of people suffer from irrational fears every day. The key to overcoming an irrational fear is to force yourself to associate it with positive emotions instead of negative ones. Every time you start thinking about the fear, try focusing on how ridiculous it might be and the actual odds of it happening.

Rational fears that are unhealthy can be the trickiest to overcome. This could be something reasonable, but the response we take to handle it is not. For example, if I decided to stop going out in public because I was afraid of getting my drink spiked, this would be a rational fear with an unhealthy response. Be willing to push yourself a little bit out of your comfort zone to manage these types of worries.

I'm often asked how I can try so many new experiences without getting scared. The truth is a big part of it has to do with how I manage the emotion itself. If I'm nervous about something (such as making a speech in front of a crowd of prominent business people or politicians), I refuse to let my anxiety get the best of me by staying focused on the task at hand. You can apply this to almost any fear by taking deep breaths and imagining yourself succeeding. Fear is a universal emotion, but you won't let it get the best of you when you learn to control it.

Try to push yourself out of your comfort zone. This doesn't mean taking stupid risks that could get you injured or killed, just ones you're comfortable trying. Remember that there's nothing wrong with being afraid. It's how you manage that fear that counts.

Protecting Yourself from Abuse

While working on your goals, you will run into people looking to bring you down. They may use various verbal, physical, sexual, or emotional abuse tactics to get what they want. Anyone looking to cause you harm or bring you down in some way is not someone who should be involved in your life anymore. It can be tempting to pretend what's happening is OK as a way to protect yourself, but you deserve better than abuse and shouldn't have to make excuses for it.

Whatever unhealthy situation you have or may find yourself in, this section is about knowing how to get out of it and begin to heal. One of my best friends was in a very abusive relationship. We'll call her Anja for this passage. While telling me the story for this section, it was hard for her to think about many things that happened to her because of the feelings that still come up, like feeling afraid, alone, trapped, and undeserving of love. She was verbally, emotionally, and physically abused during her childhood. Anja's abuser would often yell, break things, or use intimidation to try and control her. She says it took years to realize that any of this behavior was wrong because it became so 'normal.' She felt like she was the problem and deserved what was happening to her.

That's the thing about abuse. In many cases, people live in denial of it, so they don't feel attached to what happened. What began to happen is that she took all the anger unleashed on her and channeled it to her family and friends. The saying hurt people hurt people is true because abuse is a cycle, and the only way to stop it is by refusing to let it continue through you. When Anja finally saw how she was hurting the people she loved with her words, just as her abuser was hurting her, she was disgusted with herself for letting them win. She decided no matter what happened, she wasn't going to sit and take the abuse, nor was she going to let it hurt anyone else. She used to feel trapped when she was little, so she knew she needed to find a safe space to escape. She turned to the church and threw herself into learning everything she could about the Bible. Jesus was the comfort she needed because He talks about loving others no matter what and how to begin healing. This is the part of her story that gets crazy. The abuse suddenly stopped. The person saw their words and actions no longer affected her and was worried they would no longer be a part of her life. She realized that even though what happened to her was wrong, it happened for a reason. It made her stronger, pushed her towards a closer connection with God, and has driven her to help others who have suffered through the same thing.

I've noticed a common theme between people who have been abused in some way. They bottle up all the pain the abuse has caused and then spread it to others. OR they are somehow able to heal inside and let all the negativity dissipate without hurting anyone else. People like this can truly find peace with what's happened and move on to form healthy relationships with others.

I have a friend who everyone calls a "ray of sunshine" because she's able to be happy, kind to others, and loving despite the pain others have tried to cause her. People like her are so strong and brave to stand up to their abuser and not let it hurt them anymore. They've been able to take away the abuser's power by finding joy in themselves. That's what I want to teach you to be able to do. That way, no matter what comes your way in life, you'll not only be able to put a stop to it but also win by not letting it drag you down.

I want to be clear; you should never let abuse continue once you've identified it. **You need to remove yourself from the abuser both physically and mentally as soon as possible.** Find "safe spaces" where you can go, such as someone's house, a school, a room, or a church. Finding a safe space helps so much because you'll be able to get away and assess the situation better. In Anja's case, she was able to find family and friends who would look out for her. It's up to you to decide who you want to tell, but it's essential to bring at least one person you trust to help with the situation if your life isn't in danger by doing so. I had many people tell me stories of things that had happened to them. I realized how widespread abuse is and that sometimes we think it's OK just because something is familiar to us. This is not true at all. Even if a single person has to deal with being hurt by others, it is one person too many.

You deserve nothing but love and respect from others, and if that's not what you're getting, then it's time that changes. You need to be the one to change your circumstances. Find outings and activities where you can physically distance yourself and have valid reasons to leave. If you're living with the person, move out if you're able. If it's safe to do so, block all forms of communication such as social media, phone calls, and texts. You can do different activities to stay busy and improve yourself. It's also a great way to keep away from the abuser and be productive.

Mentally distancing yourself can be the most challenging but most fruitful part of healing. You can't let what they've said or done continue to affect you negatively. Find people in your life who will encourage you no matter what and other healthy support systems. You can find this through family, sports, teachers, youth or support groups, church, school clubs, and projects. By becoming a part of something bigger than yourself, you can begin the healing journey with the help of people who will have your back. Focus on yourself and achieving your goals. Recognize you can't change the past, only the future. This means you get to choose who you want to become.

There are long-term effects to abuse even after feeling at peace with yourself and what's happened. Sometimes you might find yourself forgetting the abuse over time because the brain begins to block out the painful memories. People who have dealt with abusive situations often suffer from "disassociating," which means they feel like they're not here for a short period of time. It can be terrifying because they can't escape the feeling and don't know when it will happen next. They may also deal with flashbacks where they feel like they're reliving what's happened without warning. Sometimes certain circumstances can trigger it, and other times it's random. If you suffer from any of this, you know how scary it can feel. Know you are loved and that other people understand your pain. It's not your fault, and you shouldn't feel guilty if you deal with any of this. It doesn't make you a weak person. If anything, you're stronger than most because you've survived much more than other people and still been able to succeed in life.

Do not be passive. I'm not asking you to sit and take the abuse. Instead, get out of the situation as fast and as safely as possible and work towards healing yourself. You can't change them, but you can change yourself, and sometimes that's the best option we have. Sometimes you might want to take the "easy route." For example, if you're a woman being abused by a man in your life, you might be tempted to run away into the arms of another man. This isn't the solution. You'll always be running away from someone or something until you first address what's inside your heart. Once you find inner peace, you won't feel the need to escape from everything all the time. You'll be able to face your problems head-on and solve them before they get bigger.

No one deserves to be abused. You should never shortchange yourself or tolerate toxic behavior from others. For my friend, she would feel guilty about distancing herself from the abuser because she wanted to show forgiveness. She realized that **you can show forgiveness from a distance** and that forgiving someone doesn't mean sitting by and taking abuse. Know that you are loved and deserve to be in healthy, happy relationships with other people. Focus on becoming the best version of yourself and channel all that negativity into making a positive difference.

Finally, you need to **be strong.** The most challenging part about being in an abusive situation is realizing you deserve better even if the abuser treats you like you aren't worth it. You are a talented, meaningful, unique person who is loved unconditionally by God and deserves nothing but love and acceptance. If you or someone you know is in an abusive situation, check out the contact information at the back of the book for abuse hotlines, helpful websites, and more.

DO BIG!

CHAPTER 8:

DO BIG

*"If you can dream it,
you can do it."*
—Walt Disney

You did it! You made it to the last chapter! If you've made it this far, you've proven you can set goals and achieve them. You are a driven, determined, and focused person and have what it takes to do incredible things. If you want to succeed, you can get there. Stop doubting yourself and your abilities or letting the negativity of others affect YOUR life. Only you can decide at the end of the day to succeed, and the only person who can stop you from trying is yourself. If you put in more effort than everyone else around you, there's only so much other people can do to get in your way before they give up themselves. You just have to work harder than the people trying to stop you and stay focused on your goals. If you're willing to do this, you really can achieve anything.

What kind of world would we live in if some of our most outstanding leaders had quit because people doubted them or made it hard? People like Martin Luther King Jr., Susan B. Anthony, or Mahatma Gandhi had millions of people who didn't believe in them around the world. Their critics even threatened violence or prison to stop them from achieving their goals. Yet, they persevered. You can take the pushback the world gives you as a warning to quit or as the fuel to keep going. The decision is entirely yours. Sometimes, the only difference between people who succeed and people who don't is whether they give up on themselves.

To do BIG things, you have to be willing to take the pushback that comes with it. The bigger things you accomplish in life, the more people may try and drag you down. Keep your head up, and don't stop until you get where you want to be. It won't be easy, but it'll be worth it in the end. To do BIG things in life, you have to be willing to **BET** everything on your success. I'm not talking money. Instead, be **B**old, **E**mbrace failure, and **T**hink big.

Be Bold

To do BIG things, sometimes you have to take BIG risks. That can be a part of the fun. Either way, that's what makes the achievement notable. If something were easy, everyone would have already done it. Being more daring is something you can work on and hone for the rest of your life. Having more courage comes with confidence. Some people are just born with it. Some people always enter the pool from the steps and never want to get their hair wet. Others always cannonball and jump in. Some people take life cautiously without taking too many risks. Others like experiencing life as much as possible. I certainly am at the latter, but neither is "right" or "wrong." It's your life, after all!

Remember, though, to always protect yourself. YOU have to figure out what risks you're willing to take and where you cross the line. Know yourself and your goals well enough to determine what you are and aren't willing to do. If being bolder and more proactive in your life is something you want to focus on, the key is to build up your confidence and get over unhealthy and unrealistic fears. Practice taking baby risks from time to time and trying new things. To do BIG things, you have to be bold enough to do them and confident enough to keep trying.

Embrace Failure

Often, the people who do BIG things are the ones who take risks because they aren't afraid to fail. Stop limiting yourself and your goals by learning to get up again even if you're ready to quit. It might be frustrating, and you may have to cry it out or scream into a pillow when there's a significant setback. Whatever it is, you have to get back up and try again if you want to beat the game. That's the real secret to success.

The people who fail the most are often the ones who end up succeeding. NBA legend Michael Jordan put it best, saying, "I've missed more than 9,000 shots in my career. I've lost almost 300 games. 26 times, I've been trusted to take the game-winning shot and missed. I've failed over and over and over again in my life, and that is why I succeed." There is a separation in life between the people who settle for less and throw in the towel and the ones who keep going. Which person will you be? Do you want to achieve your goals enough to keep trying even when you fail? If the answer is 'yes,' then you need to find goals that will make you wake up ready to fail, knowing that one day you won't.

If you've ever gone water skiing, you know that learning how can sometimes be a painful process. For my Water Sports merit badge in scouting, I had to learn to water ski. Every day for that merit badge, every time I lost my balance meant I slammed into the water over and over again. It hurt like heck, but every time I fell, I just had to get back up and be willing to go again. It didn't take away the bruises I had from hitting the water, the cuts from landing on debris, or the desire to quit when I didn't want to get up anymore. I felt all those things, but I knew that I had to get up and try again to achieve my goal.

At the end of the week, the entire class had quit except for my brother and me. We both earned the merit badge after being able to pass 'the wake' four times. Every other kid had dropped out days prior. They may never know the joy of water skiing and overcome obstacles because they decided to quit and take a longer lunch break. Don't use hardship as an excuse to quit. Use it as fuel to succeed.

Think BIG

To Do BIG, you have to Think BIG. Often, when people aren't successful on a large scale, it's because they don't give themselves a fair shot. If you have a goal, don't limit yourself because you're afraid of failure. Most people don't aim high enough because they don't want to disappoint themselves or others around them. You have to get over this fear if you're going to succeed. Take your goals, and don't be afraid to scale them up a bit.

When I wanted to join Scouts, I automatically knew I would go for the highest rank of Eagle. After looking at the merit badges, I decided I would aim to earn every single one as well. All you need to do when starting a goal is to choose to pursue it. From there, you can begin figuring out the logistics.

Many people believe if they do little things over time, it will add up, but unfortunately, that rarely works. Often in the United States, we are trained as children how to be employees and not employers. In school, we have to follow all the rules. Line up. Raise your hand. Go here, go there. There's not a lot of encouragement on out-of-the-box thinking. To be successful, you have to be willing to go your route in life.

Think about a person as a cashier at a grocery store who hopes to one day become a manager. They work the register year after year with the hopes of one day getting to their goal. Even if they do one day make it to that spot, there's only so much further they can go in life career-wise. What if they had decided to do BIG and start their own business instead? If that works out, the payoff could be huge, and if it doesn't, at least they'll know what works and what doesn't so they can apply it to their next effort. Some people are perfectly content working at the same grocery store at the same job, and that's great. It is a stable, respectable job. But I'm encouraging *you* to Do BIG.

To do so, take a goal you have and aim higher. If you want to get accepted into an Ivy League school, try getting into *all of them*. If you have to take the ACT, focus on getting a perfect score. If you don't fully succeed, that's OK. Have enough confidence in yourself and your abilities not to let it affect your life in the big scheme of things. Take your ambitions and pursue them, but don't limit yourself because you don't think you can do it.

You have to work on yourself first before working on your goals. To do this, it's crucial to build healthy habits that help you balance out your life.

It doesn't matter what your goals are. You need to be healthy all around to achieve what you want. Being able to build and maintain healthy habits is a huge part of working toward your goals. There are hundreds of healthy habits you can adopt right now to improve your life drastically.

Many goals require us to be in good shape as well as being able to handle the mental strain that comes with it. It doesn't matter if your plans involve sitting at a desk or not. Staying in good physical shape will help you get better sleep, stay focused longer, and even help with motivation. The same goes for mental health. If you're working on training for a sports team, it will be so much easier to learn the plays if you have a healthy mindset. It's often the little things that go unnoticed, which can later become the most significant problems. As much as we may want to focus on one or two goals solely, it can harm us in the long run. By focusing on having a more balanced set of priorities, they tend to help each other.

There are all kinds of healthy habits you can add to your routine now to help you in the long run in many of your goals. **Keep a glass of water by your bed** so when you wake up, you can start the day off right by staying hydrated. This is also a great way to lose weight, clear up acne, and even increase your energy levels. Develop an **exercise** plan and commit to it.

Curb emotional eating by keeping a food diary and working on healthy ways to manage stress. **Don't reward yourself with food**. Basic needs should never be used as a motivator. Find things to look forward to and use that as a reward instead. Take breaks to **spend time outdoors**. Just going for a walk after a long day can help you clear your thoughts and make you feel better about what's ahead. **Ignore the scale**. For years, I never had a scale in my house because my family didn't think it was a healthy way to measure yourself. Your weight can vary based on lots of factors and should not determine your self-worth. **Eat a wide variety** of food and **avoid having big meals all at once**.

Work on **boosting your confidence** by being positive, giving compliments to others, and laughing at your mistakes. **Keep a journal** of your thoughts and vent if you feel stress building. Take time to **hang out with good friends** who have your best interests in mind. **Take healthy risks** and try new things from time to time.

Every day it's a challenge to live like this. Some days you might find yourself feeling healthy all around, and other days you might feel awful and unmotivated. That's OK. We all have days where we just want to call it quits. It's on these days, though, when you keep going that you will succeed just by persevering.

Whatever your goals are in life, don't be afraid to aim high. Even if you miss, you'll still end up going further than if you just settled for less. Doing BIG things doesn't always mean becoming a celebrity, a billionaire, or an influential politician. It could be as simple as volunteering on your Saturdays at a food bank or telling a friend how much you admire her confidence. Sometimes even the littlest of things that we do in life can have a massive impact on others.

You have goals, and it's time to reach them. You are the only one who can make it happen and change YOUR life. Find out what you're passionate about and pursue it with everything you have. Spread God's love through your words, actions, and impact on others. Whatever you decide to do in life, do it to the best of your ability. My grandpa would always tell my mom that even if she worked hauling trash all day, she should still be the best trash hauler she can be. The reason is that if you refuse to tolerate laziness in yourself, you'll be able to be successful in all areas of your life by simply trying your hardest. Stop the mentality of "I can't." You CAN if you are willing to work hard and smart for it.

I believe in you and so do the people in your life who have helped you get to this point. Whatever your goals are, as small as they might seem, go out and achieve them. Do not be afraid of failure or embarrassment. Be stronger than your fears and braver than your enemies. Doing BIG is about more than the goal itself. It's about your willingness to be bold and take on the impossible. It's about pushing yourself to new levels and not stopping until you get there. It's about the impact you leave behind and whose lives you help to change. Go out and travel to that one place you've always talked about going to see. Start the business you were afraid to begin. Apply to the school of your dreams even if you might not get accepted. You can be more than you ever thought you could. You need to have faith in yourself. I believe in you. Now go out and change the world. You've got this. DO BIG.

IMPORTANT INFORMATION:

National Suicide Prevention Lifeline:
(1)-800-273-TALK
https://suicidepreventionlifeline.org

National Sexual Assault Hotline
(1)-800-656-HOPE
https://www.rainn.org

National Domestic Violence Hotline
(1)-800-799-SAFE
https://www.thehotline.org

National Human Trafficking Hotline
(1)-888-373-7888
https://humantraffickinghotline.org

ACKNOWLEDGMENTS

"Family is not always by blood. It is by heart."
—Soumen Das

Firstly, I owe everything to God for putting so many incredible people in my life. I can't ever fully thank my mom and dad enough for everything they do each day to help my siblings and me. You both have shown me what it means to show true devotion, to be selfless and loyal. I love you both so so much and want to sincerely thank you for everything you've done to be there for me. Thank you to my siblings, Harrison and Hailey, for loving me no matter what and sticking by my side through thick and thin. To my amazing grandparents, Jim and Gunn Loyd, for making life like a James Bond movie whenever we're together. I also owe a huge thank you to Jennifer Adair, Michael Adams, Jack Aitken-Smith, Léonie Aitken-Smith,

Oskar Alas, Dawn Antonis, Nancy Alvarez, Jeremy Appleton, Omar Aquil, David Ash, Adriana Bahena, Sarah Beggs, Molly Bell, Joy Bell, Robin Bentley, Mia Bickley, Matthew Blackwood, Cindy Bohn, Liam Bomkamp, Laci Booker, Matthew Bowman, Stephanie Bradbury, Chasity Brannon, Tim Brannon, Jaden Brannon, Olivia Brannon, Emma Braun, Chloe Braun, Deneige Broom, Jeff Broomell, Anne Buckle, Allison Bucko, Ruby Bucko, Travis Burgner, Nicole Burgner, Amy Butsch, Josiah Castaneda, Michelle Connor, Sarah Costello, Chiara Coves, Caitlyn Cox, Catharine Cox, Chris Crowley, Rebecca Cunningham, Julia Cunningham, Wanda Curtis, Stephen Dee, Rebecca Devoid, Michael DeWolfe, Samuel DeWolfe, Marcus DeWolfe, Chris Duran, Vanessa Echols, Lanette Edwards, James Edwards, Elena Ernst, Isabella Fancy, Gabe Ferreira, Duane Fogg, Annabelle Folvarcik, David Frank, Julie Frank, Joe George, Sabrina Gidley, Giselle Gidley, Max Gidley, Martie Godzwon, Zachary Gress, Alessandra Gallian Guimarães, Austin Guthrie, Kala Guthrie, Julie Hall, Michael Hanley, Ace Harrison, Anna Harvey, Richard Hearn, Gregg Heinsch, Luke Heinsch, Bob Higgins, Emma Hill, Andrew Hirneisen, Greg Holcomb, Greg Holcomb,

Patience Holman, Joy Holman, Mercy Holman, Seth Holman, Colleen Huddleston, Dawson Hulme, Ginny Jacobson, Jimmy Jacobson, Willie Jones, Dustin Kaczmarczyk, Luke Karvia, Cody Kavinski, Briar Kraft, Dag Kraft, Thomas Kubicki, Judith Landin, Madison Landon, Audrey Lao, Tanner Lawson, Natasha Lejan, Justin Lee, Remy De Leon, Taylor Grace Lewis, Giovanni Lopresti, Lucas Lopresti, Larry Louree, Isabelle Loyd, Karina Loyd, Kenneth Loyd, Laura Loyd, Eric Magendantz, Mia Marapao, Maserall Marcelin, Mario Martinez, Grace Melon, Harley Mergenthaler, Jordan Mergenthaler, Leah Mergenthaler, Lorenzo Mergenthaler, Karen Miller, James Moore, Steven Moore, Steve Moore, Kenneth Morgan, Emily Moyer, Chuck Mullen, Jean Nardi, Eireanna Ogden, MakennaLinn Ogdon, Brian O'Neill, Wren Parris, Nicole Parris, Madeline Peacock, Ocean Peaze, Scott Phillips, Charles Pineo, Paul Podraza, Matthew Ragan, Grace Rall, Megan Rall, Sundance Trail Dude Ranch, Vanessa Rea, Patrick Reckner, Brian Reiners, Daniela Riddle, Sean Riddle, Ricardo Rivera, Shira Rodriguez, Neviela Rodriguez, Anthony Rodriguez, Kathy Rodriguez, Anthony Rodriguez, Ileana Roman, Katelyn Ruff, Anne Russell, Aimee Sandifer, Jon Savage, Adam

Schaefon, Macy Schmitt, Richard Schultz, Melissa Schultz, Josh Schweitzer, Monica Schweitzer, Kari Schwendenman, Warren Scoville, Julia Shepherd, Brian Shields, Esther Sloop, Sarah Sloop, Warren Sloop, Noah Smith, Grant Squires, Cassi Squires, Ray Stacey, Heather Stevens, Scott Stewart, Jonathan Stout, Janell Stout, Terry Taggart, Kirsten Tesdall, Isabella Tunney, Heidi Walker, Jennifer Weymouth, Terry Wheeler, Ashton Whiffen, Freddi Wood, RJ Wood, Sammi Wood, Lexi Wood, Gabbi Wood, Trinity Wood, Rosemary Youngblood, and Amy Zentz for being such incredible people. Thank you for everything.

Q&A WITH THE AUTHOR

1. In your book, you mention traveling extensively. Where were some of the places you were able to go, and what did you learn on your trips?

Some of my favorite places I visited was The White House, Buckingham Palace, the Tower of London, Mont Saint Michael, Neuschwanstein Castle, Mount Vernon, Château de Chambord, Palace of Versailles, Eiffel Tower, Monticello, The Summer Palace, The Forbidden City, The Colosseum, Vatican City, Gardens by the Bay, Sydney Opera House, Mount Rushmore, The Golden Gate Bridge, Tokyo Disney, Leaning Tower of Pisa, La Sagrada Familia, Stonehenge, Berlin Wall, The Strip, Louvre Museum, and Niagara Falls. Each location on this list represents a culture with its own traditions, ideas, and values that gave me a new perspective on humanity. It's not the places themselves that gave me a different outlook. It's the people. All this has given me insight into the shared struggles and joys of what it means to be human. I've realized that we are more similar than we are different and that what divides us is insignificant in the big scheme of things. Sometimes when people travel, they get the feeling of how inconsequential they are. I don't feel this way. I see the ability we have to impact others and that each of us truly can make a difference.

2. Why did you write Do BIG?

I think that finding who we are and what we want can be incredibly hard to do at times. I wanted to share a bit about my journey and let people know they're not alone. I worked to create a book that was straightforward, honest, and geared toward my generation to show them how much of an impact they can have.

3. Is this book part of a series?

This is a standalone book. I am also working on a series that amplifies some of the concepts in Do BIG. To stay updated on release dates, sneak peeks, and more, be sure to check out my website hannahvholmes.com and Instagram @ hannahvholmes

4. The idea of love and acceptance is strong in your book. What about this idea moved you?

I think that one of the biggest needs and greatest solutions in the world is love. Many of the struggles we face as humans involve a lack of feeling loved and accepted. Now more than ever before, parents are busy at work trying to make a living for their children, who are often on social media trying to fill in the gaps and need for attention, acceptance, and ultimately love. I wanted to show the reader there's another way to feel loved and accepted, and it doesn't involve doing Tik Tok dances. When you achieve what God designed you to do in life, you feel fulfilled and content. I want to help my readers start working on getting to this point in their life and find acceptance within themselves first.

5. How did you come up with the title?

In society, we're often told to *think* or *dream* big. I wanted to take this concept further by urging the reader to DO Big things. After all, the first step of achieving your goals is through changing your mindset. I wanted to focus on helping people to DO outside the box and dare to be their amazing, original selves.

6. What is your favorite passage in the book and why?

My favorite passage in the book is about having a *Negative Body Image* because of how raw and personal it was to write for me. This section took dozens of rewrites before I got it to say exactly what I wanted. I knew I only had a short amount of space to make my point, and I wanted to do so as eloquently as possible. I know there's a lot of pressure on how people look, and I wanted to let you, the reader, know you have so much more value.

7. In Chapter One, you discuss the importance of having a bucket list. What are some items on your bucket list you've been able to check off?

Oh gosh, this involves some pretty random stuff! Wrapped a snake around my neck, milked a cow, watched a sea turtle lay eggs, sheered a sheep in Scotland, swam with manatees, sea turtles, sharks, stingrays, jellyfish, gone whale watching in Alaska, ridden horses in the snowy peaks of Colorado, on the beach, and in the wilderness, held a koala in Australia, a gator, a peregrine falcon, went dogsledding in Denver, partied on a private island and dove shipwrecks in the Keys, driven cars, sailed boats, gone surfing, kayaking, canoeing, flown planes, drones, rode bikes, skateboards, horses, rollerblades, ice skating, snowboarded, whitewater rafted, harvested my own honey, hiked the Appalachian trail, climbed every step of the Eiffel tower both up and down, been a mermaid at Weeki Watchi, gone snow skiing down black diamonds in Colorado, water skied in West Virginia, caught a wave surfing, survived a tidal wave in South Florida, hugged a Redwood, wrote and recorded my own song at the Country Music Hall of Fame in Nashville Tennessee, been in a commercial, modeled for Lilly Pulitzer, been on National Television, rode down the Shenandoah River in a ducky, wrote a book, built a website, starred in a play, DJ'd a party, hula danced at sunset in Hawaii, made my own perfume in Paris, done over 400 hours of volunteer work, sipped tea in Kensington Palace, caught, cooked, and ate my own fish, air boated an alligator infested swamp, rode a hot air balloon where it was first invented (Annonay, France), explored an ice caved in Austria, visited Anne Frank's attic in Amsterdam and the Auschwitz concentration camp in Poland.

8. What do you want readers to learn from this book?

You matter. You are amazing and loved just the way you are. Keep faith in your goals even when others doubt. You don't need to change who you are and what you stand for just because it may not be popular.

LIST OF ALL ONE HUNDRED AND THIRTY-SEVEN MERIT BADGES:

American Business Merit Badge
American Cultures Merit Badge
American Heritage Merit Badge
American Labor Merit Badge
Animal Science Merit Badge
Animation Merit Badge
Archaeology Merit Badge
Archery Merit Badge
Architecture Merit Badge
Art Merit Badge
Astronomy Merit Badge
Athletics Merit Badge
Automotive Maintenance Merit Badge
Aviation Merit Badge
Backpacking Merit Badge
Basketry Merit Badge
Bird Study Merit Badge
Bugling Merit Badge
Camping Merit Badge
Canoeing Merit Badge
Chemistry Merit Badge
Chess Merit Badge
Citizenship in the Community Merit Badge

Citizenship in the Nation Merit Badge
Citizenship in the World Merit Badge
Climbing Merit Badge
Coin Collecting Merit Badge
Collections Merit Badge
Communication Merit Badge
Composite Materials Merit Badge
Cooking Merit Badge
Crime Prevention Merit Badge
Cycling Merit Badge
Dentistry Merit Badge
Digital Technology Merit Badge
Disabilities Awareness Merit Badge
Dog Care Merit Badge
Drafting Merit Badge
Electricity Merit Badge
Electronics Merit Badge
Emergency Preparedness Merit Badge
Energy Merit Badge
Engineering Merit Badge
Entrepreneurship Merit Badge
Environmental Science Merit Badge
Exploration Merit Badge
Family Life Merit Badge
Farm Mechanics Merit Badge
Fingerprinting Merit Badge
Fire Safety Merit Badge
First Aid Merit Badge
Fish and Wildlife Management Merit Badge
Fishing Merit Badge
Fly Fishing Merit Badge
Forestry Merit Badge

Game Design Merit Badge
Gardening Merit Badge
Genealogy Merit Badge
Geocaching Merit Badge
Geology Merit Badge
Golf Merit Badge
Graphic Arts Merit Badge
Hiking Merit Badge
Home Repairs Merit Badge
Horsemanship Merit Badge
Indian Lore Merit Badge
Insect Study Merit Badge
Inventing Merit Badge
Journalism Merit Badge
Kayaking Merit Badge
Landscape Architecture Merit Badge
Law Merit Badge
Leatherwork Merit Badge
Lifesaving Merit Badge
Mammal Study Merit Badge
Medicine Merit Badge
Metalwork Merit Badge
Mining in Society Merit Badge
Model Design and Building Merit Badge
Motorboating Merit Badge
Moviemaking Merit Badge
Music Merit Badge
Nature Merit Badge
Nuclear Science Merit Badge
Oceanography Merit Badge
Orienteering Merit Badge
Painting Merit Badge

Personal Fitness Merit Badge
Personal Management Merit Badge
Pets Merit Badge
Photography Merit Badge
Pioneering Merit Badge
Plant Science Merit Badge
Plumbing Merit Badge
Pottery Merit Badge
Programming Merit Badge
Public Health Merit Badge
Public Speaking Merit Badge
Pulp and Paper Merit Badge
Radio Merit Badge
Railroading Merit Badge
Reading Merit Badge
Reptile and Amphibian Study Merit Badge
Rifle Shooting Merit Badge
Robotics Merit Badge
Rowing Merit Badge
Safety Merit Badge
Salesmanship Merit Badge
Scholarship Merit Badge
Scouting Heritage Merit Badge
Scuba Merit Badge
Sculpture Merit Badge
Search and Rescue Merit Badge
Shotgun Shooting Merit Badge
Signs, Signals, and Codes Merit Badge
Skating Merit Badge
Small Boat Sailing Merit Badge
Snow Sports Merit Badge
Soil and Water Conservation Merit Badge

Space Exploration Merit Badge
Sports Merit Badge
Stamp Collecting Merit Badge
Surveying Merit Badge
Sustainability Merit Badge
Swimming Merit Badge
Textile Merit Badge
Theater Merit Badge
Traffic Safety Merit Badge
Truck Transportation Merit Badge
Veterinary Medicine Merit Badge
Water Sports Merit Badge
Weather Merit Badge
Welding Merit Badge
Whitewater Merit Badge
Wilderness Survival Merit Badge
Wood Carving Merit Badge
Woodwork Merit Badge

List of Belt Ranks:
10th Gup White Belt: 2 Months
9th Gup White Belt with Yellow Stripe: 2 Months
8th Gup Yellow Belt: 2 Months
7th Gup Yellow Belt with Green Stripe: 2 Months
6th Gup Green Belt: 2 Months
5th Gup Green Belt with Blue Stripe: 3 Months
4th Gup Blue Belt: 6 Months
3rd Gup Blue Belt with Red Stripe: 6 Months
2nd Gup Red Belt: 6 Months
1st Gup Red Belt with Black Stripe: 9 Months

1st Dan (Il Dan) Black Belt: 2 Years
2nd Dan (Ee Dan) Black Belt: 2 Years
3rd Dan (Sam Dan) Black Belt: 4 Years

FOLLOW HANNAH ALONG ON HER ADVENTURES AND FOR INFORMATION ON HER UPCOMING BOOKS/SPEAKING ENGAGEMENTS:

Instagram: @hannahvholmes
Tik Tok: @hannahvholmes
Twitter: @hannahvholmes
Facebook: @hannahvholmes1
Website: hannahvholmes.com
YouTube: Hannah V Holmes

NOTES

Dreisbach, Shaun. "Shocking Body-Image News: 97% of Women Will Be Cruel to Their Bodies Today." *Glamour*, 2 Feb. 2011, www.glamour.com/story/shocking-body-image-news-97-percent-of-women-will-be-cruel-to-their-bodies-today.

Gaille, Brandon. "21 High School Sweethearts Marriage Statistics." *BrandonGaille.com*, 22 Nov. 2019, brandongaille.com/20-high-school-sweet-hearts-marriage-statistics/.

Finkelhor, D., Hotaling, G., Lewis, I. A., & Smith, C. (1990). Sexual abuse in a national survey of adult men and women: Prevalence, characteristics and risk factors. *Child Abuse & Neglect 14,* 19-28. doi:10.1016/0145-2134(90)90077-7

ABOUT THE AUTHOR

Hannah V Holmes was born in 2005 and lives in Orlando, Florida, with her family and pet rabbit. She is a motivational speaker, author, 3rd-degree black belt in Taekwondo, SCUBA diver, Student Pilot, social media influencer, and the first girl in the history of Scouting to have earned every merit badge. Hannah has traveled extensively to more than 20 countries, 40 states, and four continents and is on a mission to help people live their best life through finding internal happiness.